Ovid *Heroides*

MONMOUTH SCHOOL FOR GIRLS

NAME	FORM	DATE
mererid Jones	12C	28th June, 2018

The following titles are available from Bloomsbury for the OCR specifications in Latin and Greek, first teaching September 2016

Cicero *Pro Milone*: A Selection, with introduction by Lynn Fotheringham and commentary notes and vocabulary by Robert West

Ovid *Heroides*: A Selection, with introduction, commentary notes and vocabulary by John Godwin

Propertius, Tibullus and Ovid: A Selection of Love Poetry, with introduction, commentary notes and vocabulary by Anita Nikkanen

Seneca Letters: A Selection, with introduction, commentary notes and vocabulary by Eliot Maunder

Tacitus *Annals* I: A Selection, with introduction by Roland Mayer and commentary notes and vocabulary by Katharine Radice

Virgil *Aeneid* VIII: A Selection, with introduction, commentary notes and vocabulary by Keith Maclennan

Virgil *Aeneid* X: A Selection, with introduction, commentary notes and vocabulary by Christopher Tanfield

OCR Anthology for Classical Greek GCSE, covering the prescribed texts by Homer, Herodotus, Euripides, Lucian, Plato and Plutarch, edited by Judith Affleck and Clive Letchford

OCR Anthology for Classical Greek AS and A-level, covering the prescribed texts by Aristophanes, Homer, Plato, Sophocles, Thucydides and Xenophon, with introduction, commentary notes and vocabulary by Malcolm Campbell, Rob Colborn, Frederica Daniele, Ben Gravell, Sarah Harden, Steven Kennedy, Matthew McCullagh, Charlie Paterson, John Taylor and Claire Webster

Supplementary resources for these volumes can be found at
www.bloomsbury.com/OCR-editions
Please type the URL into your web browser and follow the instructions to access the Companion Website. If you experience any problems, please contact Bloomsbury at academicwebsite@bloomsbury.com

Ovid *Heroides*:
A Selection

VI: 1–100 & 127–164
X: 1–76 & 119–150

With introduction, commentary notes and
vocabulary by John Godwin

Bloomsbury Academic
An imprint of Bloomsbury Publishing Plc

B L O O M S B U R Y
LONDON · OXFORD · NEW YORK · NEW DELHI · SYDNEY

Bloomsbury Academic
An imprint of Bloomsbury Publishing Plc

50 Bedford Square	1385 Broadway
London	New York
WC1B 3DP	NY 10018
UK	USA

www.bloomsbury.com

BLOOMSBURY and the Diana logo are trademarks of Bloomsbury Publishing Plc

First published 2016

Introduction, commentary notes and vocabulary © John Godwin, 2016

John Godwin has asserted his right under the Copyright, Designs and Patents Act, 1988, to be identified as Author of this work.

British Library Cataloguing-in-Publication Data
A catalogue record for this book is available from the British Library.

ISBN:	PB:	978-1-47426-590-4
	ePub:	978-1-47426-591-1
	ePDF:	978-1-47426-592-8

Library of Congress Cataloging-in-Publication Data
A catalog record for this book is available from the Library of Congress.

Typeset by RefineCatch Limited, Bungay, Suffolk
Printed and bound in Great Britain

To Heather

Contents

Preface

This book is intended to assist students who are required to study this text for OCR's A-level examination in Latin in 2018 and 2019, but it can also be used by any students of Latin who have mastered the basics and who are now ready to start reading some Latin verse and developing their skills and their understanding. The notes assume that the reader has studied the Latin language roughly as far as GCSE, but the vocabulary list glosses every word in the text, and the Introduction assumes that the reader may be coming to Ovid for the very first time. The commentary seeks to elucidate the background and the literary features of this highly artistic text, while also helping the reader to understand how the Latin words fit together into their sentences.

My thanks are due above all to Alice Wright and her team at Bloomsbury who have been a model of efficiency and enthusiasm. My thanks also go to the anonymous academic referees of Bloomsbury and OCR who made many astute and helpful suggestions for improving the book. I benefited a great deal from the transatlantic assistance of Professor Peter Knox of Colorado. It is his text which is printed here and his edition of these poems has been both an inspiration and a guide as I prepared this book. He has also been generous with his advice on some tricky matters by email. All mistakes which remain are, of course, my own.

John Godwin
Shrewsbury
August 2015

Introduction

Ovid and his times

Publius Ovidius Naso was born on 20 March 43 BC in a small town called Sulmo (modern Sulmona) about 80 miles east of Rome. We know more about his upbringing than we do about that of other poets as he wrote more about himself than many poets do, and he tells us that his family was well-off but not politically active. He was sent to school in Rome – one of the signs of wealth in an age where there was no free schooling – along with his brother, and he studied public speaking (with a view to a legal and/or political career) although he was more drawn to the writing of poetry than to the composition of speeches. He was born into turbulent times: by the time of his birth Julius Caesar had been dead for a year and when he was 12 Caesar's great-nephew and heir Octavian defeated Mark Antony in the crucial battle off Actium, leaving the Roman world in the hands of a young man who was soon to change his name to Augustus and become the first of the emperors of Rome. The Roman Republic which had stood ever since the last of the kings – the infamous Tarquinius Superbus who had been expelled in 510 BC – was now subverted into a 'Principate' in which supreme power rested in the hands of the *princeps* or emperor, and freedom of speech and free elections came to be increasingly circumscribed and sanctioned. Ovid's choice of a career as a writer rather than as a lawyer or politician (or both, as was Cicero) is therefore not totally surprising seeing that he was born in an age when the scope for a lively-minded man to find the outlet for his talents in politics was inevitably limited by the regime in power. Ovid hardly ever refers explicitly to politics in his works, although it is clear from some of his less guarded lines that he might not have survived long as a politician in the imperial court.

As a young man he did what we might call the Grand Tour, travelling to Greece, Sicily and Asia Minor, and it is clear from his work that he, like most educated Romans, understood and read Greek literature in the original. His training as a lawyer would have encouraged him to compose *suasoriae* – artificial exercises in which the student composes a speech to 'try to persuade' (*suadere*) a historical figure at a critical moment, such as Sulla about to invade Rome, or Hannibal after the battle of Cannae – and we are told by Seneca (*Controversiae* 2.2.12) that he preferred this exercise to the writing of fictitious law cases (*controversiae*). This sort of imaginative work did him no harm at all as a budding writer and his composition of *Heroides* shows ample signs of having been much influenced by these student exercises. The imaginary letters from women to their absent lovers are all prime examples of cogent persuasive rhetoric.

Ovid's political career did not, then, last long and he soon devoted himself to writing poetry. He may have enjoyed the private means which other poets such as Horace did not have; or he may have continued with some business interests alongside his literary output. Literature was clearly however the focus of his career.

He began by writing love poetry in elegiac couplets: three books of *Amores* ('Loves', or 'Love-affairs') which are fully in the tradition of love-elegy, although his cheeky spirit of fun was showing already as he parodies earlier love-elegies in cases such as the sparrow of Catullus' mistress being (aptly) imitated in the 'parrot' of Ovid's Corinna. He published three books of these elegies, purporting to be love poetry told in the first person. Then he followed this with *Heroides*, fictional verse letters written from famous women of legend. All this early poetry of his was composed in the elegiac metre and it was all concerned with various aspects of love. Ovid also at some point composed a verse tragedy *Medea* which was highly acclaimed but which has not survived: this is a huge loss and would have been most interesting to compare and contrast with the portrayal of Medea in poems VI and XII of this collection as well as her character as depicted in the seventh book of his *Metamorphoses*.

Much of ancient literature was didactic in that it claimed to teach its readers lessons of one sort or another. Sometimes it was explicitly so, as in Nicander's poem *On Venomous Reptiles*, Lucretius' poem *De Rerum Natura* or Virgil's *Georgics*, and sometimes it was simply a feeling that poetry ought to educate both young and old. Ovid next produced two works which pretended to be didactic literature, but composed them in the elegiac metre of love poetry rather than the hexameters of the traditional didactic epic. *Medicamina Faciei Femineae* ('Medical Treatments for Woman's Appearance') looked at how women could maintain their appearance with drugs and potions – very much in the style of the didactic poet Nicander. We only have 100 lines surviving of this poem, but *Ars Amatoria* (the first two books of which were published in 1 BC) was a sustained experiment in applying the form of didactic poetry to the elegiac content of the life of love, instructing young men how to court women using abundant material from literature and legend, as well as giving us some vivid descriptions of ancient Rome (such as the Circus Maximus and its races). This was followed by the 'Antidote to Love' (*Remedia Amoris* (1 BC–AD 2)) which is clearly a sequel to the successful *Ars Amatoria*.

The *Metamorphoses* – a massive epic poem in 15 books telling tales of transformation of all kinds – was written before his exile in AD 8 and is perhaps the single greatest achievement of the poet. Exile was imposed on Ovid by the Emperor Augustus because of an unspecified poem of Ovid's (usually regarded as *Ars Amatoria*) and his very mysterious 'crime', which seems to have consisted in the poet witnessing something secret and which was scandalous enough to have him banished to remote Tomis (modern Constanza on the Black Sea coast of Romania) for the rest of his life. Before his exile he had also begun to write *Fasti* – a lengthy poem on the feasts and tales associated with the Roman calendar, with one book for each of the months of the year.

Once stranded in exile in Tomis he composed *Tristia* (AD 9–12) – 'Sad Things' – poems expressive of Ovid's misery in his banishment, as well as the *Epistulae ex Ponto* and the mysterious curse-poem *Ibis* (*c.* AD 10–11). For all his poetic pleading, Ovid never returned to Rome and died at the age of 60 in AD 17. It is cruelly ironic that Ovid's last works were verse letters in which he got to play the role of the abandoned figure begging for rescue from his ruler Augustus, much as he had dramatized similarly abandoned figures all those years before in the work you are now reading, *Heroides*.

Summary of the poems in the collection

Twenty-one verse letters with the title *Heroides* have come down to us in the manuscripts of Ovid – although the authorship of at least one (Poem XV) of them has been doubted.

Poem I Penelope writes to her absent husband Ulysses (Odysseus) who went to fight in the Trojan War twenty years earlier. Her house is beset with suitors urging her to choose one of them as her new husband. Even her father urges her to marry one of them, but she longs for Ulysses and writes to him just before his triumph over the suitors.

Poem II Phyllis, princess of Rhodope, has fallen in love with Demophoon (son of Theseus) who landed at her island because he needed to repair his ships. She married him, but he left her and she now vows to commit suicide.

Poem III The captive Briseis was the girl who loved Achilles and who was taken from him to live with Agamemnon after the disastrous quarrel – and Achilles' withdrawal from the fighting – which begins Homer's *Iliad*. A deputation was sent to plead with Achilles to return to battle but failed to persuade him, and Briseis here writes of her longing for her former lover/master.

Poem IV Phaedra writes to her stepson Hippolytus, bastard son of Theseus by the Amazon Hippolyta. Phaedra has become infatuated with her stepson and in the absence of her husband seeks to seduce him. She pleads her love and uses a variety of arguments to try to convince him: she points out that his father Theseus had killed her brother (the Minotaur) and abandoned her sister Ariadne (see Poem X) and had also murdered his mother. She claims that Theseus prefers the company of his friend Pirithous to both of them and proposes that they set up home together. The gods practise incest, and so it cannot be wrong. The poem is a powerful evocation of a woman in love, suddenly sharing her beloved's passion for hunting and pleading with him to rescue her from her emotional turmoil.

Poem V Oenone writes to Paris, the Trojan prince. He had been exposed on Mount Ida as a baby after his mother Hecuba, on the night before his birth, dreamed that she would give birth to a firebrand which would engulf all of Troy. The baby was brought up by shepherds and married the river-nymph Oenone. When, later on, he had judged the beauty competition of the three goddesses and was given Helen, the wife of Menelaus of Sparta, as his wife, he left Oenone.

Poem VI Queen Hypsipyle of Lemnos has formed a close relationship with Jason when he visited her island on his way to get the Golden Fleece from Colchis. She urges him to return to her.

Poem VII Queen Dido of Carthage begs Aeneas not to leave her: he has landed there on his way from Troy after the end of the war and is en route to Italy where he is destined to found a new kingdom.

Poem VIII Hermione, princess of Sparta and daughter of Menelaus and Helen, was betrothed to Orestes, the only son of King Agamemnon of Mycenae. This betrothal was overturned and her father gave her to

Pyrrhus, son of Achilles, on the grounds that Orestes was unclean after murdering his mother Clytemnestra in revenge for her murder of his father Agamemnon. Pyrrhus has taken Andromache, widow of the Trojan prince Hector, as his slave-girl and Hermione longs for Orestes to come and rescue her.

Poem IX The hero Hercules has returned home to his wife Deianeira in Trachis after sacking the city of Oechalia. She is aware that he has fallen in love with the captive princess Iole and reproaches him for his infidelity to her. In a bid to restore his love for her she has laced a garment with what she thought was a love-potion given to her by his enemy Nessus, and discovers during the poem that the love-potion was in fact a poison which kills him. She resolves to die.

Poem X Ariadne, princess of Crete, has betrayed her father Minos by helping the Athenian Theseus to slay her half-brother the Minotaur and escape from the Labyrinth. He has now abandoned her on the island of Naxos and she implores him to come back for her.

Poem XI Canace writes to her brother Macareus. These children of Aeolus (the turbulent god of the winds) had fallen in love with each other and produced a child. When Aeolus found out he was furious, had the child exposed to be eaten by wolves and sent a sword to Canace for her to commit suicide. Canace writes the letter to her brother in explanation of her fate.

Poem XII Medea writes reproaching Jason for his new marriage to Glauce, princess of Corinth. She reminds him how she had helped him secure the Golden Fleece from Colchis and hints darkly at the revenge she will enact upon him and his children.

Poem XIII Protesilaus was the leader of a platoon of soldiers going to fight in the Trojan war and was married to Laudamia. She writes to him while he is still on the way to Troy, warning him of the oracle which foretold that the first man to leap ashore at Troy would be killed instantly.

Poem XIV King Aegyptus had fifty sons, while his brother King Danaus had fifty daughters. Aegyptus wanted his sons to marry their cousins, but Danaus had heard an oracle which foretold his death at the hands of a son-in-law and so the large family fled to Argos. Aegyptus' clan followed them and persuaded them to carry out the wedding, but Danaus instructed all his daughters to murder the new husbands on their wedding night. Hypermnestra, the oldest of the daughters of Danaus, refused to kill her husband Lynceus and was thrown into prison by her furious father, from where she writes this letter.

Poem XV Sappho, the famous lyric poetess of Lesbos, writes to her beloved Phaon, the ferryman who had been given irresistible sex-appeal by Aphrodite after he offered her free transport over the sea. Phaon has now left her and she expresses her longing for him and her thoughts of throwing herself into the sea.

Poems XVI and XVII This is a pair of poems between Paris, the Trojan prince and former lover of Oenone (see Poem V) and Helen, the Queen of Sparta, given to Paris by Aphrodite as his reward for giving the goddess the golden apple in the famous 'Judgement of Paris'. Poem XVI sees Paris ask Helen to run away with him as his wife. In Poem XVII Helen at first refuses, but as the poem goes on she warms to the idea.

Poems XVIII and XIX A pair of poems between Hero and Leander. In Poem XVIII Leander writes across the Hellespont to his illicit lover Hero stating that he will venture over the stormy seas as he cannot bear their separation any longer. In Poem XIX Hero replies, reciprocating his affection, but urging him not to risk his life on the sea.

Poems XX and XXI Cydippe, a rich and noble woman on the island of Delos, had been tricked into promising to marry the impoverished Acontius, but had then been promised to another man by her father, and this new marriage had only been delayed by Cydippe suffering a fever. In Poem XX Acontius writes to her suggesting that the fever has been sent by the goddess Diana, in whose temple she had unwittingly sworn her love. In Poem XXI Cydippe writes back that Acontius had ensnared her by trickery, but that her fever will

not abate and she fears that the gods really are forcing her to carry
out her vow.

Heroides

These poems are a wonderful mixture: they combine love-elegy (as
had been written by Catullus, Gallus, Tibullus and Propertius, as well
as Ovid himself in *Amores*) with the more funereal lament typical of
the elegiac genre. They express love and desire as did the poets of love-
elegy in the previous and current generation, but this time they are an
exploration of longing for the other over an expanse of space, and (in
Poems I–XV) they are composed exclusively from the point of view
of the deserted woman. They are epistolary in form but quite unlike
the philosophical *Epistles* of Horace, composed in rugged didactic
hexameters and published shortly before *Heroides*. Ovid himself (*Ars
Amatoria* 3.345–6) claimed that he invented the literary genre of the
elegiac letter and recommends it as reading material for his female
audience. They are fictional speeches conveying what these voiceless
women might have said if they had had the chance, obeying
Thucydides' famous dictum (*History of the Peloponnesian War* 1.22)
that he aimed to reproduce 'what would have been necessary on each
occasion', but of course allowing the poet to indulge his imagination
to the full as well as his rhetorical skills.

In the later uses of the epistolary form – such as Gabriel de
Guilleragues' *Letters of a Portuguese Nun* (1669), Samuel Richardson's
Pamela (1740–1) and *Clarissa* (1748–9), Goethe's 1774 novel *Die
Leiden des Jungen Werther* or Laclos' 1782 novel *Les Liaisons
Dangereuses* – the sequence of dated letters allows us to see the single
story in frozen moments of time, each one a part of the temporal
jigsaw fitting together into a linear narrative but with each letter
limited by the knowledge and feelings available at the time of its

purported composition. Ovid here similarly freeze-frames the narrative, capturing the moment at which the heroine is stuck in her plight. Catullus (64.50–266) had written *his* version of Ariadne as a poetic reconstruction of a picture, a narrative unfrozen from a static image on a bedspread in what is called an *ecphrasis*, a moving film made out of a still picture. Ovid does the opposite, looking at one moment of the story and exploring the full implications of the awful scene. He chooses the epistolary form to lock the moment into a single glimpse of a heroine, as she looks backwards in time and outwards to her departing lover, but is unable to look forward to see what lies ahead. These poems are self-consciously letters rather than transcripts of speeches, and so for example Dido's letter to Aeneas (Poem VII) can be (even) more eloquent than her speeches to him in Virgil's *Aeneid* 4, because she has had time to write and revise it rather than relying on improvised inspiration on her feet. The literary quality of these poems, like that of all Ovid's poetry, is archly self-conscious and ironic.

In the first place the poems refer to each other ('intratextually') and are clearly meant to be read as a collection. The final six poems in the collection are 'doubles' where (for instance) Paris writes to Helen in Poem XVI and then Helen writes back to Paris in Poem XVII. The cross-reference is obvious in these double-poems, but there is also reference between Oenone's letter to Paris in Poem V and the words of Paris and Helen in poems XVI and XVII. In the 'single' poems the references can be more subtle: Hypsipyle in Poem VI is troubled by the apparent triumph of Medea in taking her place in Jason's affections, only for this to be nicely overturned in Poem XII where the same Medea, now herself abandoned, utters the same sort of reproaches as her predecessor to the same faithless lover. In Poem IV.116 Phaedra refers to her husband Theseus abandoning her sister Ariadne and thus looks forward to Poem X: and the same Theseus is the angry father-figure of Demophoon of Poem II. The same names crop up again and again and the world of the *Heroides* is in all senses a narrow one.

In the second place the heroines occasionally draw attention to the artificiality of the genre with deliberate references to the 'letter-writing' process taking place – see for instance Phaedra's explanation (IV.7–14) that she has to write a letter as she is tongue-tied when they meet, or else Ariadne's precarious attempt to write on a wax tablet while clinging to a wet rock (X.136–140). Similarly, Ariadne's words (X.3–4) 'I am sending you the words you are reading' remind us that she will have to find some convenient means of delivering a letter – from a desert island! At the end of the same poem, however, Ariadne fantasizes (X.150) about Theseus coming too late and finding only her bones for him to take back for burial, and this grim realism makes us realize that the artificiality of the epistolary genre is in this case a means of underlining the desolation of the women concerned. These women have nothing except illusory means of reaching their lovers: and the fact that letters almost always reach their addressee and achieve their aim of being 'conversation with absent friends', as Seneca tells us (*Letters* 55.9), makes their desolation all the greater. This same device is used even in cases such as that of Penelope where she is by no means isolated on Ithaca with 108 suitors nagging her night and day as she awaits the return of her absent husband Ulysses. Here (I.59–62) the heroine presses her letters onto every passing mariner to take to Ulysses in a futile quest for his attention.

The poems are concerned a great deal with writing and reading: think for instance of poor Cydippe, entrapped by being led to read aloud a written vow to wed Acontius in Poem XX. In broader terms these poems are excellent examples of 'intertextuality' in that they also refer self-consciously and deliberately to earlier literary texts. These heroines are not, after all, invented figures but rather women well-known from Greek and Roman literature and so anybody reading Poem I (for instance) would likely know that Ulysses is in fact about to come home, and the letter can be reliably 'dated' by internal references to the night before the slaying of the suitors. In Poem VI there is similar dramatic irony as we know from Poem XII and from Euripides' *Medea* that Medea's victory over Hypsipyle is going to be short-lived and the foreign poisoner will soon be in the same position as the jilted queen. In Poem X we know that Bacchus is going to rescue Ariadne (as Ovid himself tells us in *Ars Amatoria* 1.527–64 and Catullus had described in 64.251–64) and so there is nice dramatic irony in both poems as the audience is better informed than the characters and can smile at the suffering as it is soon about to end. In other poems the dramatic irony is less comfortable: we know, for example, from Sophocles' tragedy *Women of Trachis* that Deianeira is going to be bitterly disappointed when Hercules puts on her robe in Poem IX. Poem XI marks a real descent in mood: Homer introduces the incest of the children of Aeolus in his *Odyssey* (10.5–12) without batting an eyelid. The tale was unpacked and embellished in later tragedies such as Euripides' (lost) play *Aeolus* and it seems that Ovid has developed this tragic version of the tale into a very dark world of incest and infanticide (see section on the 'moral landscape').

Poem IV is a letter from Phaedra to her stepson Hippolytus and the intertextuality here is particularly striking, as Phaedra's language reminds us now of Dido (7–8), now of Sappho (20), now of her own character in Euripides' *Hippolytus* (41–2). Her mode of argument uses rich analogies from the natural world in the manner of didactic poetry (e.g. 21–4) and even at one point (35–6) echoes the words of Catullus' beloved as reported by him in Poem 70. She is using every trick in the book(s) to seduce her stepson with this very literary love-letter. Her arguments to persuade the young man into a relationship with his father's wife remind us of the sophistic 'Wrong Argument' in Aristophanes' *Clouds* 1079–82 or Euripides' *Trojan Women* 948–50 (an argument which was part of Plato's moral objection to tragedy (*Republic* 391E)). More commonly in love-elegy it is a male lover who seeks to seduce a married woman and mocks her dolt of a husband (cf. Ovid *Amores* 1.4; Catullus 83) but this poem takes the traditional portrayal of Phaedra as both scheming and charmingly amoral and appropriates the male language of seduction for a female speaker. Euripides famously wrote two versions of the story: one (now lost) where Phaedra was a wicked seductress, and one (the surviving play *Hippolytus*) where she was the innocent victim of the wrath of Aphrodite and forced to fall in love against her will. Interestingly, Ovid has his cake and eats it in that he has the 'nasty' Phaedra say the sort of things which the 'nice' Phaedra cannot bring herself to say (IV.10) but which she can put into a letter. He makes full use of the psychologically disturbed Phaedra of the later play (such as her sudden passion for hunting) but lets her speak as one in the grip of a passion which affects her heart but not (apparently) her ability to forge articulate arguments (just as he had also done in the case of Scylla in *Metamorphoses* 8.44–80). He took the suicidally mute woman of Euripides' later play, whose moral world was being destroyed, and gave her a voice. In doing so he challenges our assumptions on many levels, using typically male chat-up patter in the mouth of an older woman to advocate both adultery and incest and invoke divine precedent for both.

Poem VII has been much discussed as the intertextuality here features the most iconic work of Roman literature, Virgil's *Aeneid*. Dido writes to her departing lover Aeneas, and here the poet draws on the speech which Virgil puts into her mouth in the same position in *Aeneid* 4.305–30. One can easily see where Ovid has used and where he has adapted his 'source', but of course this is no simple plagiarist rehashing of his illustrious predecessor but rather a way of revisiting the text. By the time Ovid writes this poem Dido has already 'lived' this experience in Virgil's poetry and has learned in the meantime. Where, for instance, Virgil (*Aeneid* 4.168) tells us it was nymphs who howled at her 'wedding' in the cave, Dido now corrects this statement and tells us that it was the grim Furies (VII.96). What makes it even more interesting is that Virgil himself was writing in a tradition, and his account of Dido draws on Apollonius Rhodius' account of Medea in his *Argonautica*, and Apollonius in turn drew on earlier sources, such as tragedy, so that we have Ovid reading Virgil reading Apollonius reading earlier writers.

✝   All Roman poets were 'learned' (*doctus*) and they all wrote in a conscious tradition in which imitation was expected and the challenge was to put a new spin on old material, striking the right balance between tradition and originality. Ovid is, of course, something of an innovator throughout his career, for all that he uses earlier material: his 'epic' (*Metamorphoses*) was no hackneyed mythological or historical saga (such as Juvenal mocks in his *Satires* (1.1–14)) but a wonderful cycle of stories all linked by the theme of 'transformation', a theme highly appropriate to a poet who transforms words in the air into pictures in the mind.

The moral landscape

The *Heroides* are not always comfortable reading. Phaedra is urging her stepson to commit incest in Poem IV. Poem XI shows us a baby being thrown to wolves by its grandfather because it has been incestuously conceived between brother and sister, which makes the adultery of Paris and Helen in Poem XVI seem comparatively innocent, and the string of abandoned wives and lovers (Dido, Sappho, Oenone and so on) positively normal behaviour. These poems show us the murder of husbands by their wives in poems IX and XIV, the murder of a mother by her son in Poem VIII, along with dismemberment of a brother by a mother (Medea), who will later murder her children (Poem XII), and the forcing of a girl to kill herself by her own father in Poem XI. There is the use of entrapment to wed a rich girl in poems XX and XXI and repeated complaints that men make vows and then break them, 'treacherous' being a common epithet flung at the absent beloved. All of this suggests a Gothic world of grotesque moral abnormality in which everything is allowed and misery abounds, with poetry left as the one thing which can linger as being 'good'. The use of argumentation, which makes the 'weaker case' appear the 'stronger', is something that the Sophists in fifth-century BC Athens had practised – see for instance Gorgias' wonderful *Defence of Helen* – and that Ovid will have learned in his rhetorical training as a young man. If, after all, one can 'justify' incest and adultery, then one has learned the craft of oratory, and Ovid in many parts of his work shows a combination of rhetorical content married to poetic form, often using the arguments of the law courts in the pursuit of love. This is not however enough to answer the critics of Ovid's moral nihilism, such as the one who dismissed the poet's *Art of Love* as 'all art and no love'. Plato in the *Gorgias* had argued that rhetoric has to apply moral thinking to prevent it becoming a weapon in the hands of the wicked. Is it a fair accusation to say that Ovid is exploiting his material, reducing moral and tragic cases to entertainment and a veneer of flashy speech? Brecht's comedy *Arturo Ui* was accused of turning the Nazi regime into comic entertainment and so making light of human suffering. Could the same be said of a Phaedra luring a stepson into bed, or a sister offering herself to a brother? Are relationships which today would be termed abusive being prettified into poetry and so rendered acceptable by a veneer of amoral charm? Is that why the poet chose to retreat into the bookish world of earlier literary figures rather than making up his own 'heroines', using what has been called 'textual intercourse' as a mask of propriety for what is pulp fiction?

One answer to this is that the immorality does not make any of them happy and so is not being recommended as a lifestyle choice. Ovid is less concerned about passing judgement than asking us to 'peek over the shoulder' of a distressed woman, as Anderson nicely put it. Our own moral feelings are explored in these cases of individual needs and desperate situations, and if we are so sure that Phaedra is wrong, then we only need to find the flaws in her argument. We hear her words and hear them as what a deranged woman would say, not as a call to action for ourselves. Literature has to be realistic, and this involves looking at the irrational and the disturbed sides of human nature, exactly as when we watch tragedies on stage.

✳ Ovid shows enormous interest in human psychology throughout his career, from the aspects of love shown in his early *Amores*, through the kaleidoscope of weird people in *Metamorphoses*, right up to his own confused articulacy in *Tristia*. These poems invite pity as well as empathy for the heroines who are all trapped either in their geographical location or else in their own psychological hamster-wheel.

Ultimately, Ovid is a writer rather than a moralist or a psychologist. He is concerned to give us literature that will make us smile, cry, think and feel. If his poetry succeeds in making his audience argue and rage, either with or against these sad women, then he has done his job extremely well.

The metre of the poem

Latin poetry is written in a fairly rigid system of metres, all of which in turn rely on the pattern of heavy and light syllables, and the metre of the *Heroides* is the 'elegiac couplet' in which a 'hexameter' alternates constantly with a 'pentameter'. This was the metre used in love poetry and also in epigrams and funeral laments.

The hexameter line consists of six divisions usually called 'feet'. The first four of these can be either 'dactyls' (–∪∪) or 'spondees' (– –), where the symbol '–' indicates a heavy syllable and the symbol '∪' a light one. It is usually assumed that a heavy syllable is equivalent to two light ones. The fifth foot of a hexameter is almost always a dactyl and the final foot is always one of two syllables, and so it is either a spondee or else a trochee (–∪).

Syllables which contain a diphthong (i.e. a pair of vowels pronounced together, such as *au, ae*) or else a long vowel are heavy syllables, and syllables where a short vowel is followed by two (or more) consonants are also made heavy – although if the second consonant is 'liquid' such as 'l' or 'r' (for instance in the word *patris*) then this need not happen. The two consonants do not have to be in the same word as the vowel for this to take place (e.g. VI.12 *necem dextra* where the (short) final 'e' of *necem* is followed by the initial 'd' of *dextra* and so lengthened).

Vowels are either long or short by nature and sometimes vary with inflection (e.g. the final -*a* of *mensa* is long in the ablative case, short in the nominative) and one must be aware that the letter 'i' may be a vowel in some places (*nix*) and a consonant in others (*iam*). The quantity of vowels is marked with a '–' symbol in good dictionaries such as Morwood's *Pocket Oxford Latin Dictionary*.

In cases where a word ending with a vowel (or a vowel + m such as *iustam*) is followed by a word beginning with a vowel or 'h', the two syllables usually merge ('elide') into a single syllable, as VI.31 where *utque animus* is read as *utq'animus*. Where this ought to happen, but does not, the device is called 'hiatus' and is unusual: see VI.15 *o ego*.

Thus a 'typical' hexameter line will run like the first line of Poem VI:

–UU/ –UU /– //UU / –UU / –UU / – –
litora/ Thessali/ae// redu/ci teti/gisse ca/rina

where the // sign shows the 'caesura', i.e. the word-break in the middle of a foot. This usually happens in the third foot after the initial heavy syllable, but can also come in the middle of the two short syllables in a dactyl; in such cases there is often a further caesura in the fourth foot, as in line VI.5.

The pentameter is made up of five feet but the line is always scanned in two halves of 2.5 feet. The feet are (as in hexameters) made up of dactyls or spondees but the central pause or caesura is invariable and marks the division of the line into its two constituent halves. The final single syllable may be either long or short ('anceps') and is marked here with 'x' to indicate this.

The line thus breaks down as follows:

–UU / – – / –// –UU / –UU / x
diceris/ aura/tae// vellere/ dives o/vis.

Latin words also have a natural stress accent (which works as in the same way as English words such as táble, tomáto, fúrniture), whereby most words of more than one syllable were stressed on the penultimate syllable, or on the antepenultimate if the penultimate were a short vowel. Thus the first line of Poem VI would be spoken:

lítora Thessáliae réduci tetigísse carína

but 'scanned' metrically as:

lítora/ Théssali/áe reduc/í teti/gísse car/ína

Quite how the two ways of reading Latin verse blended or competed is unclear, but it is clear that in hexameters there is a tendency for the stress accent of the spoken word and the metrical 'beat' or 'ictus' to conflict in the earlier and middle parts of the line but to coincide at the end. Look for instance at X.9, where the metrical beat is marked by **bold** type and the ´ sign indicates the speech stress:

incértum vígilans ác sómno lánguida móvi

Further reading

The most accessible translations of the *Heroides* are those in the Penguin Classics series by Isbell (London, 1990) or else the Loeb Classical Library (2nd edition: translated by Showerman and revised by Goold 1989).

There is an excellent edition of *Heroides* I, II, V, VI, VII, X, XI, XV (Knox) and of *Heroides* XVI–XXI (Kenney) in the Cambridge Greek and Latin Classics series.

Secondary reading on the *Heroides* includes:

Anderson, W. S. 'The *Heroides*', in: *Ovid* Binns (ed.) (London, 1973), pp. 49–83.

Jacobson, H. *Ovid's Heroides* (Princeton, 1974).

Lively, G. *Ovid: Love Songs* (London, 2005).

Spentzou, E. *Reading Characters Read: Transgressions of Gender and Genre in Ovid's Heroides* (Oxford, 2003).

Verducci, G. *Ovid's Toyshop of the Heart: Epistulae Heroidum* (Princeton, 1985).

See also these articles (all available through JSTOR):

Barchiesi, A. 'Future Reflexive: Two Modes of Allusion and Ovid's "Heroides"', *Harvard Studies in Classical Philology*, Vol. 95 (1993), pp. 333–65.

Farrell, J. 'Reading and Writing the "Heroides"', *Harvard Studies in Classical Philology*, Vol. 98 (1998), pp. 307–38.

Hinds, S. 'Medea in Ovid: Scenes from the Life of an Intertextual Heroine Author(s)', *Materiali e discussioni per l'analisi dei testi classici*, No. 30 (1993), pp. 9–47.

Kennedy, D. F. 'The Epistolary Mode and the First of Ovid's "Heroides"', *Classical Quarterly*, 34 (1984), pp. 413–22.

Myers, S. 'The Metamorphosis of a Poet: Recent Work on Ovid', *The Journal of Roman Studies*, Vol. 89 (1999), pp. 190–204.

For more general books on Ovid as a writer see:

Wilkinson, L. P. *Ovid Recalled* (Cambridge, 1955).

Hardie, P. (ed.) *The Cambridge Companion to Ovid* (Cambridge, 2002), especially Chapter 13 (Kennedy: 'Epistolarity: the *Heroides*', pp. 217–32).

For a brief guide to the scansion of Latin hexameter poetry see:

Kennedy B. H. *The Revised Latin Primer* (London, 1962), pp. 204–5.

Text

Poem VI: Hypsipyle to Jason

litora Thessaliae reduci tetigisse carina
    diceris auratae vellere dives ovis.
gratulor incolumi, quantum sinis; hoc tamen ipsum
    debueram scripto certior esse tuo.
nam ne pacta tibi praeter mea regna redires,   5
    cum cuperes, ventos non habuisse potes;
quamlibet adverso signatur epistula vento.
    Hypsipyle missa digna salute fui.
cur mihi fama prior quam littera nuntia venit,
    isse sacros Marti sub iuga panda boves,   10
seminibus iactis segetes adolesse virorum
    inque necem dextra non eguisse tua,
pervigilem spolium pecudis servasse draconem,
    rapta tamen forti vellera fulva manu?
o ego si possem timide credentibus ista   15
    'ipse mihi scripsit' dicere, quanta forem!
quid queror officium lenti cessasse mariti?
    obsequium, maneo si tua, grande tuli.
barbara narratur venisse venefica tecum
    in mihi promissi parte recepta tori.   20
credula res amor est. utinam temeraria dicar
    criminibus falsis insimulasse virum!
nuper ab Haemoniis hospes mihi Thessalus oris
    venerat et tactum vix bene limen erat,
'Aesonides', dixi, 'quid agit meus?' ille pudore   25
    haesit in opposita lumina fixus humo.
protinus exsilui tunicisque a pectore ruptis
    'vivit? an,' exclamo, 'me quoque fata vocant?'

'vivit,' ait timidus; timidum iurare coegi.
vix mihi teste deo credita vita tua est. 30
ut rediit animus, tua facta requirere coepi:
narrat et aeripedes Martis arasse boves,
vipereos dentes in humum pro semine iactos
et subito natos arma tulisse viros;
terrigenas populos civili Marte peremptos 35
inplesse aetatis fata diurna suae.
[devictus serpens. iterum, si vivat Iason,
quaerimus; alternant spesque timorque vices.]
singula dum narrat, studio cursuque loquendi
detegit ingenio vulnera nostra suo. 40
heu, ubi pacta fides? ubi conubialia iura
faxque sub arsuros dignior ire rogos?
non ego sum furto tibi cognita; pronuba Iuno
adfuit et sertis tempora vinctus Hymen.
an mihi nec Iuno, nec Hymen, sed tristis Erinys 45
praetulit infaustas sanguinolenta faces?
quid mihi cum Minyis? quid cum Tritonide pinu?
quid tibi cum patria, navita Tiphy, mea?
non erat hic aries villo spectabilis aureo,
nec senis Aeetae regia Lemnos erat. 50
certa fui primo (sed me mea fata trahebant)
hospita feminea pellere castra manu;
Lemniadesque viros nimium quoque vincere norunt.
milite tam forti fama tuenda fuit.
urbe virum vidua tectoque animoque recepi. 55
hic tibi bisque aestas bisque cucurrit hiems.
tertia messis erat, cum tu dare vela coactus
implesti lacrimis talia verba suis:
'abstrahor, Hypsipyle; sed dent modo fata recursus,
vir tuus hinc abeo, vir tibi semper ero. 60
quod tamen e nobis gravida celatur in alvo,
vivat, et eiusdem simus uterque parens.'
hactenus, et lacrimis in falsa cadentibus ora

cetera te memini non potuisse loqui.
ultimus e sociis sacram conscendis in Argo. 65
illa volat; vento concava vela tument.
caerula propulsae subducitur unda carinae;
terra tibi, nobis aspiciuntur aquae.
in latus omne patens turris circumspicit undas;
huc feror, et lacrimis osque sinusque madent. 70
per lacrimas specto, cupidaeque faventia menti
longius assueto lumina nostra vident.
adde preces castas inmixtaque vota timori,
nunc quoque te salvo persolvenda mihi.
vota ego persolvam? votis Medea fruatur? 75
cor dolet atque ira mixtus abundat amor.
dona feram templis, vivum quod Iasona perdo?
hostia pro damnis concidat icta meis?
non equidem secura fui semperque verebar,
ne pater Argolica sumeret urbe nurum. 80
Argolidas timui: nocuit mihi barbara paelex!
non expectata vulnus ab hoste tuli.
nec facie meritisque placet, sed carmina novit
diraque cantata pabula falce metit.
illa reluctantem cursu deducere lunam 85
nititur et tenebris abdere solis equos;
illa refrenat aquas obliquaque flumina sistit;
illa loco silvas vivaque saxa movet.
per tumulos errat passis discincta capillis
certaque de tepidis colligit ossa rogis. 90
devovet absentes simulacraque cerea figit
et miserum tenues in iecur urget acus,
et quae nescierim melius. male quaeritur herbis
moribus et forma conciliandus amor.
hanc potes amplecti thalamoque relictus in uno 95
impavidus somno nocte silente frui?
scilicet ut tauros, ita te iuga ferre coegit:
quaque feros angues, te quoque mulcet ope.

adde quod ascribi factis procerumque tuisque
  se iubet et titulo coniugis uxor obest.   100

*101–26: Medea will get all the credit and your parents would not
approve of her – let her find a husband from her own people. Fickle
Jason, you let me down. If you are looking for a noble wife, I am very
well connected and you will have Lemnos as a dowry. I have given birth
to your twins who look like you: I almost sent them to you as tiny
ambassadors, but I feared their stepmother.*

Medeam timui: plus est Medea noverca;   127
  Medeae faciunt ad scelus omne manus.
spargere quae fratris potuit lacerata per agros
  corpora, pignoribus parceret illa meis?   130
hanc tamen, o demens Colchisque ablate venenis,
  diceris Hypsipyles praeposuisse toro.
turpiter illa virum cognovit adultera virgo,
  me tibi teque mihi taeda pudica dedit.
prodidit illa patrem; rapui de caede Thoanta.   135
  deseruit Colchos; me mea Lemnos habet.
quid refert, scelerata piam si vincit et ipso
  crimine dotata est emeruitque virum?
[Lemniadum facinus culpo, non miror, Iason;
  quamlibet ignavis iste dat arma dolor.]   140
dic age, si ventis, ut oportuit, actus iniquis
  intrasses portus tuque comesque meos,
obviaque exissem fetu comitante gemello
  (hiscere nempe tibi terra roganda fuit),
quo vultu natos, quo me scelerate videres?   145
  perfidiae pretio qua nece dignus eras?
ipse quidem per me tutus sospesque fuisses,
  non quia tu dignus, sed quia mitis ego.
paelicis ipsa meos implessem sanguine vultus,
  quosque veneficiis abstulit illa tuos.   150
Medeae Medea forem! quod si quid ab alto

iustus adest votis Iuppiter ille meis,
quod gemit Hypsipyle, lecti quoque subnuba nostri
   maereat et leges sentiat ipsa suas;
utque ego destituor coniunx materque duorum,   155
   cum totidem natis orba sit illa viro.
nec male parta diu teneat peiusque relinquat:
   exulet et toto quaerat in orbe fugam.
quam fratri germana fuit miseroque parenti
   filia, tam natis, tam sit acerba viro.   160
cum mare, cum terras consumpserit, aera temptet;
   erret inops, exspes, caede cruenta sua!
haec ego, coniugio fraudata Thoantias, oro.
   vivite devoto nuptaque virque toro!

Poem X: Ariadne to Theseus

mitius inveni quam te genus omne ferarum;
   credita non ulli quam tibi peius eram.
quae legis, ex illo, Theseu, tibi litore mitto,
   unde tuam sine me vela tulere ratem.
in quo me somnusque meus male prodidit et tu,   5
   per facinus somnis insidiate meis.
tempus erat, vitrea quo primum terra pruina
   spargitur et tectae fronde queruntur aves.
incertum vigilans ac somno languida movi
   Thesea prensuras semisupina manus.   10
nullus erat! referoque manus iterumque retempto,
   perque torum moveo bracchia: nullus erat!
excussere metus somnum; conterrita surgo,
   membraque sunt viduo praecipitata toro.
protinus adductis sonuerunt pectora palmis,   15
   utque erat e somno turbida, rupta coma est.
luna fuit; specto, si quid nisi litora cernam.
   quod videant oculi, nil nisi litus habent.
nunc huc, nunc illuc, et utroque sine ordine, curro;
   alta puellares tardat harena pedes.   20
interea toto clamanti litore 'Theseu!'
   reddebant nomen concava saxa tuum,
et quotiens ego te, totiens locus ipse vocabat;
   ipse locus miserae ferre volebat opem.
mons fuit: apparent frutices in vertice rari;   25
   hinc scopulus raucis pendet adesus aquis.
ascendo (vires animus dabat) atque ita late
   aequora prospectu metior alta meo.
inde ego (nam ventis quoque sum crudelibus usa)
   vidi praecipiti carbasa tenta Noto.   30
ut vidi indignam quae me vidisse putarem,
   frigidior glacie semianimisque fui.
nec languere diu patitur dolor; excitor illo,

excitor et summa Thesea voce voco.

'quo fugis?' exclamo; 'scelerate revertere Theseu!   35

    flecte ratem! numerum non habet illa suum!'

haec ego: quod voci deerat, plangore replebam.

    verbera cum verbis mixta fuere meis.

si non audires, ut saltem cernere posses,

    iactatae late signa dedere manus;   40

candidaque imposui longae velamina virgae,

    scilicet oblitos admonitura mei.

iamque oculis ereptus eras: tum denique flevi.

    torpuerant molles ante dolore genae.

quid potius facerent, quam me mea lumina flerent,   45

    postquam desieram vela videre tua?

aut ego diffusis erravi sola capillis,

    qualis ab Ogygio concita Baccha deo;

aut mare prospiciens in saxo frigida sedi,

    quamque lapis sedes, tam lapis ipsa fui.   50

saepe torum repeto, qui nos acceperat ambos,

    sed non acceptos exhibiturus erat,

et tua, quae possum, pro te vestigia tango

    strataque quae membris intepuere tuis.

incumbo, lacrimisque toro manante profusis   55

    'pressimus' exclamo 'te duo: redde duos!

venimus huc ambo; cur non discedimus ambo?

    perfide, pars nostri, lectule, maior ubi est?'

quid faciam? quo sola ferar? vacat insula cultu.

    non hominum video, non ego facta boum.   60

omne latus terrae cingit mare; navita nusquam,

    nulla per ambiguas puppis itura vias.

finge dari comitesque mihi ventosque ratemque:

    quid sequar? accessus terra paterna negat.

ut rate felici pacata per aequora labar,   65

    temperet ut ventos Aeolus, exul ero.

non ego te, Crete centum digesta per urbes,

    aspiciam, puero cognita terra Iovi.

[Handwritten annotations: "Regret" (left margin, line 60); "no way out" (line 62); "tricolon : building up", "anticlimax = pathos", "personification" (lines 63–64); "narrative – undeniable" (line 66); "the ultimate destination vs Naxos." (lines 67–68)]

et pater et tellus iusto regnata parenti
  prodita sunt facto, nomina cara, meo.   70
cum tibi, ne victor tecto morerere recurvo,
  quae regerent passus, pro duce fila dedi,
tum mihi dicebas: 'per ego ipsa pericula iuro,
  te fore, dum nostrum vivet uterque, meam.'
vivimus, et non sum, Theseu, tua, si modo vivit   75
  femina periuri fraude sepulta viri.

77–118: You should have killed me along with the Minotaur. I will die here, mauled by savage animals. I face danger on sea and on land and cannot go through the sky. If only none of this had ever happened, if only I had not helped you against the Minotaur. No wonder you defeated the Minotaur – you are more savage than he. Treacherous sleep, the winds and your perjured oaths all betrayed me.

Ergo ego nec lacrimas matris moritura videbo,
  nec, mea qui digitis lumina condat, erit?   120
spiritus infelix peregrinas ibit in auras,
  nec positos artus unguet amica manus?
ossa superstabunt volucres inhumata marinae?
  haec sunt officiis digna sepulcra meis?
ibis Cecropios portus patriaque receptus,   125
  cum steteris turbae celsus in ore tuae
et bene narraris letum taurique virique
  sectaque per dubias saxea tecta vias,
me quoque narrato sola tellure relictam:
  non ego sum titulis subripienda tuis.   130
di facerent ut me summa de puppe videres!   133
  movisset vultus maesta figura tuos.
nunc quoque non oculis, sed, qua potes, aspice mente   135
  haerentem scopulo, quem vaga pulsat aqua.
aspice demissos lugentis more capillos
  et tunicas lacrimis sicut ab imbre graves.
corpus, ut impulsae segetes aquilonibus, horret

litteraque articulo pressa tremente labat.   140
non te per meritum, quoniam male cessit, adoro:
  debita sit facto gratia nulla meo,
sed ne poena quidem. si non ego causa salutis,
  non tamen est cur sis tu mihi causa necis.
has tibi plangendo lugubria pectora lassas   145
  infelix tendo trans freta longa manus.
hos tibi, qui superant, ostendo maesta capillos.
  per lacrimas oro, quas tua facta movent,
flecte ratem, Theseu, versoque relabere velo!
  si prius occidero, tu tamen ossa feres.   150

Commentary Notes

Heroides VI

The speaker is Hypsipyle, the queen of Lemnos, addressing her departed lover Jason. Jason had been told by his uncle Pelias that he would only gain the throne of Iolcus if he fetched the Golden Fleece from Colchis. His ship the Argo set sail and landed at Lemnos en route: other accounts tell us that he stayed a few days – Ovid has him stay for two whole years – and in that time he developed a close relationship with Hypsipyle. He left her distraught when he had to move on to Colchis and she here voices her anguish both at his leaving and even more at his acquisition of a new 'wife' in the form of Medea. She has now heard of his successful acquisition of the Golden Fleece and his happy return to Thessaly and pours out her lonely disappointment.

1–2 **Thessaliae:** Thessaly is where Jason came from: he was allegedly brought up by the centaur Chiron in the countryside of Thessaly after his place as king of Iolcus had been usurped by his uncle Pelias. **reduci** (from *redux*) agrees with **carina** and means 'returning': *carina* literally means 'keel' but here as often is synecdoche for the entire ship. **dives** here is used with the ablative case ('rich in') and there is a nice touch in the transferring of the golden colour from the fleece to the whole animal. The effect of the couplet is harshly reductive: Hypsipyle has heard about Jason from others, not from him ('you are said') and he is reported to have 'touched' the shore with his 'keel' – but that is enough to ensure his wealth (*dives*) and Hypsipyle's anguish. The heroic exploit of removing the Golden Fleece is downgraded with the final word *ovis* ('sheep' or 'ram'): hardly a terrifying enemy to face.

Hypsipyle does not name herself until line 8 and only in line 25 does she refer to Jason with a patronymic title. The effect is twofold: the speaker cannot bring herself to name her former lover, and the reader is expected to be able to work out the story from the heavy clues (Golden Fleece, sowing of teeth).

3–4 **gratulor** ('I congratulate') always takes a dative and is possibly sarcastic here; it is undercut by the qualifying **quantum sinis** ('so far as you allow me'), as Jason has broken off contact with her and so her congratulations are difficult to deliver and would not be well received. **incolumi** is dative and here is 'proleptic', meaning '[in that you are] safe', once again being a faint jibe as it implies that Jason was hard pressed to avoid being killed. The construction of **certior esse** is interesting: *certiorem facio* is common in Latin for 'I inform' and so the passive *certior factus* means 'informed': understand *factus* with *certior esse*, taking **scripto tuo** as ablative of instrument ('by means of a written text from you').

5–6 The meaning is: 'you may have not had the winds needed – although you wanted to visit me – to let you go home past my kingdom', but Ovid cleverly starts with the last part and introduces it with a *ne* + subjunctive ('to prevent you from . . .') which then ends up meaning: 'your excuse for not coming, even though (*cum*) you wanted to, is possibly (*potes*) . . .'. In other words, Hypsipyle anticipates an excuse and refutes it. She adds a further touch of bitterness in the phrase **pacta tibi** (*regna*), which suggests that her kingdoms were 'pledged as a marriage gift' to him (cf. 117 *dos tibi Lemnos erit*).

7 Jason may have had to take a different route home if the winds were not favourable, but he could have sent a letter (which would have awaited favourable winds to be delivered). **signatur** is interesting: it means the 'sealing' of a letter and represents more than the mere

writing of one. The reason is perhaps that a queen such as Hypsipyle expects a formal sealed document – and the word also feeds into the irony that the letter is sealed but the union is broken. **quamlibet** is concessive (cf. 140) going with **adverso**: 'however adverse the wind'.

8 Hypsipyle names herself as subject of the first person verb **fui** in a haughty statement. **dignus** here takes the ablative (as at 146) – she is worthy of 'a greeting sent'. This is the *'ab urbe condita'* construction in which a noun and past participle together throw most stress on the verb in the participle: so here the phrase means 'the sending of greetings'. *salve* in Latin commonly means 'hello' and so the noun *salus* (literally: 'health' or 'wellbeing') means 'the wishing of health'. There is a further point here in the word order: the juxtaposition of **Hypsipyle missa** is suggestive of the 'dismissal' of the queen and **digna salute** suggests that she is worthy to thrive (and not to pine, as she is doing).

9 In answer to the obvious objection (how does she know he has reached home?) Hypsipyle explains that it was 'rumour' (**fama**) rather than a 'letter' (**littera**) which came to her. The series of accusative + infinitive indirect statements in lines 10–14 are all dependent on the verb of speaking implicit in **nuntia**. The queen poses an indignant question here ('why?') rather than merely stating the facts of the rumour.

10 'Cattle sacred to Mars' which 'went under the curved yoke' refers to the fire-breathing bulls with which Jason had to plough a field as part of his task in Colchis to procure the Golden Fleece from its king Aeetes. No other source mentions Mars in this connection, but the reference makes the story both more heroic (as Mars was the god of war) and also almost sacrilegious as these were cattle sacred to a god (much like the cattle of the Sun-god in Homer's *Odyssey* 12, whose

misuse cost the lives of Odysseus' men). Describing the yoke as 'curved' may seem an otiose epithet but it adds to the sense of 'crooked' which is at the heart of Hypsipyle's argument.

11 **virorum** is a surprise at the end of a line taken up with conventional agriculture: 'cast the seeds and there sprang up a crop of – MEN!' Once Jason had ploughed the field with the fire-breathing bulls he had to sow the teeth of a dragon in it and then fight the men who sprang up fully armed from the earth. Hypsipyle interestingly uses the word 'seeds' (**seminibus**) for the teeth as part of the agricultural imagery of **segetes**. Jason allegedly succeeded in this by getting the armed men to fight one another and so kill themselves. **adolesse** is a syncopated form of *adolevisse* and the shortened form here is apt for the instantaneous growth of the men.

12 The death did not need Jason's strong right hand (**dextra**) as he used trickery on them rather than direct fighting, throwing stones amongst the soldiers to confuse them and cause them to turn on one another. The language here is perfect: *dextra* often also connotes 'trust' or 'fidelity' especially of contracts (cf. how Dido laments the *dextra fidesque* which Aeneas feigned (Virgil *Aeneid* 4.597)), and so here Hypsipyle manages to insinuate that Jason had no need of a literal *dextra* in this case and had not shown her any metaphorical *dextra* either. **in** + accusative here means 'for the purpose of their killing'.

13 The line is framed with the enveloping presence of the unsleeping (**pervigilem**) dragon: note how *vigil* means 'awake' and is intensified here with the prefix *per-* (as in *per-territus*). **spolium** usually means 'spoils' of war and the fleece was certainly that: but in this case the word bears its original meaning of 'hide' and the overall effect is something like the English use of the word 'scalp' to mean both 'skin'

and also 'trophy'. The line is notable also for the preponderance of sibilants in *spolium pecudis servasse,* appropriate in the case of a snake.

13–14 Line 13 sets up the problem (there was an unsleeping dragon/ snake guarding the fleece) and line 14 shows how 'nonetheless' (**tamen**) the deed was accomplished. *fulvus* is 'tawny', often used of lions, boars, eagles and gold. The use of the plural form **vellera** for a single fleece has the effect of amplifying the achievement, as is also brought out by the adjective *forti* (sc. *manu*).

15–16 **o ego**: the phrase, with its use of *o* and the (unnecessary) personal pronoun along with the hiatus between the two words, is highly emotional. The adverb **timide** goes with the verb in the participle **credentibus** – and **ista** is the object of that participial verb: 'to those who were afraid to believe those things'. The subjunctives **possem** and **forem** (= *essem*) are both imperfect tense, showing an unreal conditional in present time: 'if I were now able to say ... I would be'. *quanta* denotes here 'how grand' and is again surprising coming from a queen – but then it also supports her thesis that Jason's betrayal and lack of communication have reduced her status and her self-esteem.

17–18 There is a strong contrast here between **officium** ('duty') and **obsequium** ('indulgent attention'). Hypsipyle regards Jason as her husband and so his absence means that his duty has 'ceased' (**cessasse** short for *cessavisse*) – the point being amplified with the adjective *lenti* ('sluggish') agreeing with *mariti*. The word *officium* (as used of a husband) suggests the duty to procreate; and *lentus* is elsewhere used of sexual unresponsiveness. We thus have Hypsipyle effectively acknowledging that her sex-life with Jason is over; but that she is happy to bear that if only she can belong to him. The feminine possessive pronoun **tua** here means 'your [girl/wife]' and **maneo** shows her clinging on to the past. *obsequium* denotes 'indulgence, compliance' and gives us the English word 'obsequious': the paradox here is that Hypsipyle will regard the bare minimum of being called 'his' to be a sign of positive attention and affection (amplified by the adjective **grande**), even though he has abandoned his 'duty'.

19 **barbara** indicates non-Greek and is a big theme in the legend of Medea through the ages. Hypsipyle is outraged that her place in Jason's bed has been given to one who is not even Greek. **venefica** means originally 'poisoner' (*venenum* = poison/noxious substance or deed) and here means 'witch'. **narratur** continues the theme of gossip as Hypsipyle's only source of information: cf. *diceris* (2), *fama* (9); but the word *narratur* suggests further that the tale of Medea is already the stuff of legend and excitement.

20 Medea has been **recepta** (taken) **in parte tori** (in a part of the bed which was) **promissi** (promised) to Hypsipyle. Notice that *promissi* agrees with *tori* and strongly states that Hypsipyle was promised the whole bed in marriage to Jason, not just a share of it: once again (see 163n.) Hypsipyle lays claim to a marriage which may not have happened.

21 'Love is (a thing (**res**) which is) quick to believe'. The queen becomes sententious and shows that she is aware of her own weakness in this respect. The idea that lovers are quick to credit stories about their beloved is well-known and works both ways of course: a lover might idealize his beloved or else (as here) be quick to think the worst. **utinam** + subjunctive indicates a wish: 'I wish I could be said to be . .', and once again the theme of what is said (**dicar**: cf. *narratur* in 19) is strong in her mind. **temeraria** indicates 'rash' or 'impulsive' and so the same Hypsipyle who agrees that love is quick to believe the worst (*credula*) is also one to hope that she is jumping to false conclusions (*temeraria*).

22 The terms here are legal ones: **crimina** are charges of a criminal nature, while *insimulo* means 'I accuse'. **virum** here has its common sense of 'husband' rather than merely 'a man' and backs up the statements of line 20 that theirs was a marriage.

23 The source of her information was a nameless Thessalian: his origins are made clear by the double geographical referents of **Haemoniis** and **Thessalus**. Haemonia was actually just an area in Thessaly but the name was commonly used for Thessaly as a whole: here it allows the poet to repeat himself without using the same word twice, a device known as *variatio*. The messenger came from the same 'shores' (**oris**) which Jason had touched in line 1. A **hospes** is a guest and also a stranger. This tale reminds us of the succession of strangers who came to Ithaca in Odysseus' absence and regaled his lonely wife Penelope with stories of her husband's imminent homecoming (cf. e.g. Homer *Odyssey* 14. 379–89).

23–5 The normal pattern for Greek hospitality was to receive the stranger with food and drink and shelter before asking anything of him: Hypsipyle's impatience is such that she cannot wait to observe the proprieties. The impatience is also brought out by the lack of a connective *cum* to join the main verbs *venerat . . . tactum erat* with *dixi* in 25. The first word Hypsipyle speaks is Jason's name in patronymic form: the suffix *–ides* means 'son of' and Aeson was Jason's father. This is either because she cannot bear to speak his name or else to draw attention to his status, as one monarch speaking of another in solemn regal terms. Her language is hardly formal, however, and shows her very human passion: *quid agis?* is colloquial Latin for 'how are you?' and *meus* means 'my dear'.

25–6 The guest is embarrassed. First of all Ovid tells us this (**pudore**), and then he shows us the proof (he hesitated (**haesit**) and kept his eyes fixed on the floor). For the inability to speak due to embarrassment and anxiety cf. Aeneas' reaction to the message from Mercury in Virgil's *Aeneid* 4.280 (*vox faucibus haesit*). **opposita … humo** means 'on the ground in front of him': **lumina** (literally 'lights') is commonly used for 'eyes' and stands here as an accusative object of the participle **fixus**, so that the whole phrase means: 'fixing his eyes on the ground facing him'.

27 If Hypsipyle's questions in line 25 could have sounded casual, her response to his silence is passionate in the extreme: 'at once' she leapt up – just as she had spoken without delay in lines 24–5 – and tore her clothing in grief. For the stripping of garments in a state of grief and anger cf. Catullus 64.63–70, Homer *Iliad* 22.468–70: for a queen to behave in this manner in front of a stranger shows a high degree of grief. There is also a suggestion (as in Catullus' account of Ariadne) that this is a form of futile sexual signalling to the absent beloved.

28 'Is he alive – or [if he is dead, then] must I die too?' The self-immolation of the widow would be grotesque and absurd in the context and the phrasing is equally melodramatic: 'the fates are calling me also' sounds like a parody of itself.

29 Ovid uses effective repetition of the verb **vivit** and then brilliantly makes use of polyptoton in **timidus; timidum** to stress the anxiety of the man, further enhanced by the choice of *coegi* at the end of the line ('I compelled him'). The timidity has been shown in the man's inability to look Hypsipyle in the eye (26) and she takes his diffidence for deceit and forces him to take an oath (*iurare*) which involved calling the gods to witness (*teste deo* in 30).

30 Hypsipyle cannot bring herself to believe that Jason is alive because this means that he has rejected her. His death would after all explain his silence and maintain her dignity.

31 **rediit** has an unusual long final syllable here: it was so pronounced in archaic Latin and later writers used this on occasions. *animus* is the 'heart' as opposed to the 'mind' (*mens*) or soul (*anima*) and here means 'my courage'. Hypsipyle will now be regaled with an excited account of what Jason has done, an account which is nicely ironic: the stranger is entertaining his host with sensational stories of heroic deeds, not perhaps realizing that he is also wounding her heart as he does so (*vulnera nostra* 40).

32 **boves:** for the cattle of Mars cf. 10n. Here the cattle have the impressive compound adjective **aeripedes** ('bronze-footed') in the manner of epic poetry (cf. *terrigenas* in 35) and the heroic term is effectively juxtaposed with *Martis*. **arasse** is a syncopated form of *aravisse* (from *aro*).

33 The 'viper' in **vipereos** was the dragon whose teeth Jason had to sow in the ground which the bulls had ploughed.

34 The speed of the action is effective and shown in three consecutive stages: these beings are (1) born suddenly (**subito natos**), at once (2) bear arms (**arma tulisse**), and are (3) fully grown men (**viros**).

35 Jason managed to get the warriors to kill each other and the speaker describes this in terms of civil war (**civili Marte**, with *Mars* (god of war) metonymic for 'war') as the earth-born men are all from the same dragon-parent, with an epic compound adjective **terrigenas** to enhance the effect of heroic conflict. The 'earth-born' men are so-called as they sprang from the sown soil: it is a nice touch that they are born (*natos*) and die (*peremptos*) in the same couplet, quick in art as in life, a point reinforced in *diurna* in the next line. The number of these men is not known, but the speaker exaggerates the heroic conflict with the plural *populos* ('peoples').

36 **implesse** is short for *implevisse* from *impleo*. Again the language is grand: not just 'they died' but 'they fulfilled the one-day fate of their life'. The speaker is clearly enjoying his task as is made clear by his increasingly soaring rhetoric. The juxtaposition of **aetatis fata** is emphatic, and the applying of **diurna** ('lasting one day') to *fata* is unusual and striking.

37–8 These lines are bracketed as their authenticity is seriously in doubt. If genuine, they show an interestingly novel use of 'telegram-style' in *devictus serpens* ('dragon defeated') standing alone with no verb. The content of the couplet tells us little that we do not already know: but there is a nice psychological touch with Hypsipyle's alternation of fear and hope along with her repeated (*iterum*) request to hear that Jason is alive. *alternant . . . vices* means 'change places' and neatly envelops the juxtaposed *spesque timorque* which brings out the instant alternation of the one and then the other.

39 **singula** means 'each individual thing'. **studio cursuque loquendi** is a good example of a 'hendiadys' where two aspects of an action are seen together: *studio* indicates 'enthusiasm' and *cursu* denotes 'speed' and so the two together come to mean 'in the excited rush of his speech'.

40 The speaker 'undresses' Hypsipyle's 'wounds': the phrase recalls the *tunicis . . . ruptis* in 27 and is a wonderful metaphor for how the news of Jason's success exposes her vulnerability – for love as a 'wound' cf. Virgil's Dido (*Aeneid* 4.1). *ingenio . . . suo* has the literal sense 'with his intelligence' but here has the undertone that he does so by his innate ability and so has this effect without meaning any harm.

41 **heu ubi** is again (like 15) an emotional hiatus to open the rhetorical question. 'where is . . .?' here means effectively 'what has become of

that …?' *fides* is often used of marital fidelity but denotes 'trust' in general. *pacta* recalls line 5 (see note there), and the poet becomes more specific in the term *conubialia iura* which can only refer to marriage rights.

42 **fax:** the torch was a standard feature of a wedding ceremony, so the word 'torches' (*taedae*) could mean (by metonymy) 'wedding' (e.g. 134, VIII.35, Catullus 64.302): here the word is well chosen as the same torch could also light a funeral pyre (*rogos*) and Hypsipyle's point is precisely that her experience was more suited to the latter than the former and so the torch was 'more fit to go under a pyre which was to burn' (*arsuros* is the future participle of *ardeo*).

43–6 The queen claims that their marriage was no illicit affair but that she had the full benefit of divine witness in the form of Juno, Roman goddess of marriage, as 'matron of honour' and Hymen wearing the right garb: the phrasing here is reminiscent of the 'marriage' in the cave in Virgil *Aeneid* 4.165–72. Hymen was the child of the Muse Urania and was the personified god of marriage: the name was called out in wedding songs such as Catullus 61. Hypsipyle then asserts that the presiding deity was in fact one of the Furies.

43–4 **furtum** literally means 'theft' and is often used of a clandestine illicit love-affair ('stolen' from the rightful spouse). *cognita* means 'known' but has the sense of carnal knowledge here as at 133 and so virtually means 'sexual partner'. **sertis tempora vinctus** means 'his brows (*tempora*) bound with wreaths': as at 26, the verb in *vinctus* governs the retained accusative *tempora*.

45–6 The couplet forms a tricolon crescendo (not Juno, not Hymen, but rather the Fury) where the third element is the longest and occupies the whole of line 46. **faces** picks up *fax* from line 42 and gives neat closure to this section. The Erinyes were the Furies – also known as 'Eumenides' and 'Dirae' – born from the blood of the mutilated primeval god Uranus. They avenged crimes and especially crimes of bloodshed within the family, especially the murder of a parent. (Hypsipyle had not allowed the murder of her father Thoas, and her language here almost suggests that she might as well have killed the old man as she is being punished all the same).

Furies were female and the best known were Tisiphone, Megaera and Allecto. Here the nameless Fury is aptly described as 'bloody' (**sanguinolenta**) and 'grim' (**tristis**): for their use of torches cf. Allecto's throwing of the torch of anger into the breast of Turnus in Virgil *Aeneid* 7.456–7. The torches are described as **infaustas**, which means 'ill-starred, inauspicious': the passage reminds the reader of the grim prophecy of the Fates at the marriage of Peleus and Thetis (Catullus 64. 323–81).

47–8 Another strong and elegant rhetorical question in the form of a tricolon crescendo, with repetition of *quid cum?*. The 'descendants of Minyas' was an alternative title for the Argonauts as it was said many of them were descended from the daughters of Minyas who was a Boeotian hero. 'Triton's pine-tree' means the ship Argo, as 'Tritonis' was an epithet applied to Athena, at whose bidding and with whose help the ship was built from pine-wood (cf. Catullus 64.1, Euripides *Medea* 1–4). **Tiphys** (from Boeotia) was the helmsman of the ship, chosen here perhaps because he was said to have died after navigating the voyage there and so seen as a symbol of the ill-omened venture. Hypsipyle addresses him in apostrophe – a device common in epic where the narrator speaks directly to a character in the tale in the second person (e.g. Homer *Iliad* 16.20, Virgil *Aeneid* 4.408) and which is fitting for this heroic tale.

49 Hypsipyle argues with Tiphys; he had no reason to stop at Lemnos as Lemnos did not have what the Argo was seeking. Her language is

deliberately scathing in tone and rhythm: note the way the Golden
Fleece becomes a 'ram' whose fleece is a 'shaggy growth' (**villo**) and
how the final two syllables of **aureo** have to be scanned as a single
syllable (a practice known as 'synizesis'), which has the effect here of
making her sound less controlled.

50 The debunking goes on: Hypsipyle ridicules King Aeetes as an 'old
man' (although he was not) and she indignantly points out that the
old man did not rule in Lemnos – she did!

51–2 The construction of **certa** + infinitive (with the sense 'determined
to …') is not uncommon in Ovid (cf. *Heroides* VII.7) but is less
common elsewhere. Hypsipyle once again invokes her fates (cf. 28)
as the agents of her life in a mirror of the Stoic idea that we are
'dragged' by fate if we do not follow willingly (cf. 59), and so on the
surface the lines mean 'I should have driven them out but my fates
decreed otherwise'. *traho* also means 'attract' however, and so we have
a nice paradox that her fates both 'dragged' her to disaster and also
'drew' her to Jason – a sense neatly countered by the infinitive **pellere**.
There is a nice clash of ideas ('oxymoron') in the phrase **hospita castra**
as enemy camps are a surprising 'guest' to have; but the phrasing is
reinforced by the juxtaposition of *hospita feminea* (looking after
guests is women's work) and then *castra manu* (an army camp is the
place for action).

53 **Lemniades:** the women of Lemnos had indeed killed men in the
past: when the women of Lemnos had neglected to worship Aphrodite,
the goddess had made them stink and their husbands had gone to the
Thracian mainland for fresher women. In revenge the Lemnian
women killed all the men – and their Thracian mistresses – on the
island (with the single exception that Hypsipyle did not kill her father
Thoas), thus producing the *urbs vidua* we see in 55. The totality of the

slaughter is behind Hypsipyle's **nimium quoque** ('even too much')
here and **norunt** (= *noverunt* perfect tense of *nosco* taking the infinitive
vincere ('they knew how to overcome')). Notice also the juxtaposition
of *Lemniadesque viros,* pitting the women against the men verbally as
in life.

54 The line literally means: 'my reputation was to-be-guarded (**tuenda**)
by soldiery so strong' and so means 'I should have let such strong
soldiers (i.e. the women) look after my reputation'. The instrumental
ablative (**milite . . . forti**) is unusual but makes eminent sense here.
Hypsipyle could have protected her *fama* or 'good name': cf. Dido's
mourning the loss of her *pudor* and *fama prior* (Virgil *Aeneid* 4.321–
2). The line is also notable for the harsh alliteration of 'f', expressive of
her contempt.

55 **urbe . . . tecto . . . animo:** there is a brilliant escalation in this line
whereby Hypsipyle took Jason into (1) the city (2) her home and
finally (3) her heart, with each of the three limbs governed in syllepsis
by the one verb *recepi.* She does not name him: in the situation it
was shocking to take any *virum* into the city. *viduus* means 'widowed'
and these women were of course widows by their own actions: the
totality of the slaughter meant that the city as a collective whole was
'widowed'.

56 Jason might have only stayed a few days, or else he might have
arrived towards the end of the sailing season, stayed over one winter
and then left in the spring: but in fact he stayed for two whole years,
suggesting that his stay was determined by more than mere practical
necessity. The length of his stay is well conveyed by Hypsipyle's use of
the seasons counted out, which elongates the phrasing to mirror the
length of time; and their happiness in this time is well suggested by
the verb *cucurrit* – the time 'ran' quickly.

57 **coactus** is sardonic in the context: after staying two whole years Jason had decided he was 'forced' to go away. In the traditional account he was compelled by Hercules who refused to remain with the ship unless they set sail – but in the traditional account they did not stay so long either. Hypsipyle does not say who or what compelled Jason to go from here, leaving us to infer that he was claiming compulsion when there was none. The term 'harvest' (**messis**) indicates that Jason left in the summertime and also hints at the harvest of children which she later on tells him she has borne (lines 119–20).

58 Literally: 'you filled out words like this with their tears' is a remarkable expression and highly compressed: she means 'you filled your eyes with suitable tears as you spoke words like this'. **suis** is accusing Jason of hypocrisy – the tears belong to the words and both are generated actively by the speaker (*implesti* is a strong indicative verb). **implesti** is a shortened form of *implevisti* from *impleo*, and *talia* looks forward to the speech which Hypsipyle now quotes back at him.

59–62 Hypsipyle quotes Jason word for word (cf. 64n.) in a grim reminder of the promises he made – and broke.

59 **abstrahor** is aptly in the passive voice, indicative of the speaker's belief that he has no choice over this – rather like Aeneas' *Italiam non sponte sequor* (Virgil *Aeneid* 4.361) – and says that he can but hope (with a wishful iussive subjunctive *dent*) that he will return, giving the responsibility for the return to 'fate'. He thus absolves himself of responsibility both for going and also for (not) returning.

60 Jason now switches to the active voice to promise his devotion to her, calling Hypsipyle by her name and repeating **vir** (here meaning 'husband' as at 22) in emphatic position at the start of each half of the

pentameter line. He expresses a commitment to eternal (**semper**) marriage to her.

61–2 Jason now turns to the child Hypsipyle may be carrying in her 'pregnant womb'. The sex of the child was not known (hence the neuter *quod*) and its presence is 'hidden' (**celatur**) but it comes from Jason himself (*e nobis*) in line with the common ancient theory that the child arose entirely from the father and the mother's role was restricted to incubating the seed planted there by the father. **vivat** is no empty wish – childbirth and infancy were dangerous times and perinatal mortality in the ancient world was high: Cornelia, for instance, who was the mother of the Gracchi, had twelve children of whom nine died in childhood. Jason expresses the wish to share the parenting, putting this elegantly with the singular **uterque parens** being also the subject of the plural verb **simus**: *eiusdem* does not mean 'the same' here but picks up the theme of the hexameter line and adds to it: 'may we also both be a parent to it'.

63 **hactenus** means 'so far' and indicates that that is all he said before breaking down in tears and being unable to speak further. Hypsipyle's doubts as to his sincerity are clearly made in **falsa** and also hinted at in **non potuisse** – he could think of nothing else to say as he had run out of excuses. **lacrimis … cadentibus** is an ablative absolute construction ('with tears falling').

64 **memini** is significant, showing that Hypsipyle does not forget anything – and so he cannot lie to her about what happened – and also showing how important these words were to her. *cetera* (literally 'the rest') is also somewhat scathing: 'the rest of the speech you were going to make', suggesting that it would not have come from his heart but from his memory.

65–6 **ultimus:** being the last to board the ship showed (an affectation of) reluctance to leave; the ship is called **sacram** ('sacred') because the goddess Athena played a large part in its construction (see 47–8n.) but the word may be sardonic here ('your holy ship') as suggesting that Jason used the divine status of the Argo to justify leaving her. The ship 'flies' (**volat** is a nice metaphor) as the crew are rested and also happy to leave: there is more than a touch of bitterness in the verb here as also in the word **sociis**, suggestive of Jason's happy band of men leaving his unhappy wife behind. **Argo** here is a Greek form of the accusative case. The prompt blowing of the wind backs up the notion that the ship was blessed with divine favour (*sacram*) and Ovid nicely shows us the wind blowing in its effect: 'the billowing sails swell with the wind'.

67 This is a 'golden line', with the form: adjective – adjectival participle – verb – noun – noun. The elegance of the Latin evokes the smooth and effortless gliding of the ship, with both the participle (**propulsae**) and the verb (**subducitur**) in the passive voice and the verb suggesting that the waves are 'drawn away from under' the keel (**carinae**) as it is 'driven along' (*propulsae*) by the wind. *carinae* must be dative case and is an example of the 'dative of separation'.

68 The one verb **aspiciuntur** governs both halves of the pentameter, and the nouns and pronouns are arranged in a neat ABBA chiasmus of *terra – tibi – nobis – aquae*. This has the effect of placing the two human agents together in ironic juxtaposition while also separating the land from the water as far as possible, with the two nouns framing the line.

69 When Hypsipyle could not see the Argo from the shore she rushes to the 'tower', which must have been a lighthouse, 'exposed in all directions' and 'surveying the waves'. The *turris* manages to do what

Hypsipyle longs to do – to see far out to sea. Note the personification of the tower here.

70 After a series of longer clauses in the preceding lines, **huc feror** is staccato and expressive of her sudden impulsive dash to the tower reminiscent of Andromache's rush to the walls to see her husband Hector in Homer *Iliad* 22.460–63. The volume of her tears is enough to wet her bosom (**sinus**) as well as her face (**os**): contrast Jason's tears only falling onto his face in 63. *-que . . . -que* meaning 'both . . . and . . .' is an epic feature (cf. 164) and heightens the grandeur of this weeping queen.

71–2 Ovid has told us that Hypsipyle is looking out to sea (68) and that she weeps: he picks up both ideas here, giving us the effective image of her looking through her tears (which ought to restrict her ability to see) but being so keen (**cupidae menti**) that her eyesight could see further than usual (**longius assueto**). Her eyes were 'favouring an ardent mind' and so supporting her ardour with enhanced vision.

73–4 **adde** is often used in didactic poetry ('consider also' e.g. Lucretius 4.1121): here it makes Hypsipyle's words more insistent and hectoring. Once again she presents herself as free of all blame (she calls her prayers *castas*) and as piously praying for Jason's safety. A *votum* was a prayer safeguarded with a promise of action to be undertaken if the prayer was answered favourably: these were often made in fear during a storm at sea and resulted in the dedication of sailors' goods in the temple (e.g. Virgil *Aeneid* 12.768–9). Such 'vows' had to be fulfilled (**persolvenda**) by the person praying – even when (as here) the object of the prayers (Jason's safety) would no longer benefit the worshipper as he had moved on. The scansion of the lines demands that the 'v' in *persolvenda* is pronounced as the vowel 'u' resulting in the dactylic rhythm *pērsŏlŭ/ēndă*. This device is known as 'diairesis': *persolvam* in 75 is scanned without the diairesis.

75 **vota:** Hypsipyle now comes to a new point: her prayers will only benefit the 'other woman' in Jason's life, Medea, who dominates Hypsipyle's thoughts for the remainder of this poem. Note the pair of indignant rhetorical questions here both beginning with a part of the word *votum* and with balanced phrasing leaving the verbs to the end of each three-word phrase. The verbs are deliberative subjunctives: 'am I to fulfil my vows? Is Medea to enjoy the benefit of the vows?' Medea was the princess of Colchis who helped Jason in his successful quest of the Golden Fleece: she fell in love with him and they fled from Colchis together, settling finally in Corinth where Jason abandoned her (as he has abandoned Hypsipyle) for the daughter of the king. Medea (in Euripides' play) in revenge murders the king, the princess and then her own children to punish her errant husband.

76 The mixture of emotions is well conveyed in this line with pain (**dolet**), anger (**ira**) and love (**amor**) blended together and overflowing (**abundat** deriving from *unda* showing the tide of her passion and apt here in the context of the lover sailing away).

77–8 A further pair of rhetorical questions on the theme of 'why should I do this?'. The gifts (**dona**) will be the ones promised in the *vota* made for Jason's safety: and **feram** is nicely indignant – am I (a queen) to have to carry these things? There is a neat paradox in the second half of 77: she has lost him (which normally indicates death) even though he is alive. A **hostia** was a sacrificial victim slaughtered as an offering to the gods: Hypsipyle uses the appropriate terms for this – the animal is struck (*icta*) and then 'falls down' (*concidat*) – and the surprise is in the term 'for my losses' as one would expect such a sacrifice to be made when loss had been avoided. **damnum** is a legal term and shows the queen speaking in authoritative language (cf. *pacta* in 5, *fraudata* in 163).

79–82 Hypsipyle had always feared that she would be supplanted by a Greek woman – only to be replaced in fact by a 'barbarian mistress' (**barbara paelex**).

79 **equidem** means 'I in fact' and introduces an aside here. *securus* means 'free from *cura*' and so 'safe' or 'untroubled by anxiety'. We now see a different side to Hypsipyle: she was not secure in Jason's affections and was always (**semper**) worried that he would be married off to a Greek woman of his father's choosing.

80 **nurus** is a daughter-in-law and the phrasing of the line strongly suggests that Jason's father would make all the arrangements and 'produce a daughter-in-law from a Greek city'. *Argolicus* here simply means 'Greek' rather than specifically 'from the Argolid': there is a nice suggestion in the phrasing that the captain of the Argo should get a wife who was *Argolica*. There is a lot of assonance in this line: of 'a' in the first half and of 'u' in the second; the pleasing euphony is going to be broken in the next line with the invasion of the *barbara paelex*.

81 Ovid neatly juxtaposes the two verbs (**timui: nocuit**) for effect and leaves the devastating term to the end of the line. *barbarus* means 'non-Greek' and carried obvious pejorative overtones of being uncivilized and fit to be enslaved, while *paelex* means a 'concubine' or 'mistress'. Hypsipyle considers herself to be Jason's legitimate wife and so any other partner can only be a *paelex*. The contempt voiced in the phrase is tinged with apprehension as Hypsipyle goes on to list Medea's formidable magic powers in the following lines.

82 The language is metaphorical: Hypsipyle has not been physically harmed and Medea is only an enemy in love rather than in war. The terms are however suitable for a queen in charge of a state.

83–94 Hypsipyle describes Medea's powers in lurid detail: perhaps to warn Jason against being tricked by a love potion (93–4) and generally to let him know what sort of woman he has become involved with – and also to raise her own morale as this has not been a fair contest if her opponent has such an unfair advantage in terms of power and if her lover has indeed been bewitched.

83 The line makes up a tricolon of 'merits': Medea is no better looking (**facie**) than anybody else and she is not superior in her 'services' (**meritis**) but she has knowledge of 'spells' (**carmina**).

84 'She crops the dread fodder with her enchanted scythe' is a wonderfully evocative line: **cantata** picks up the magic power of song from *carmina* in 83 but is here applied to the 'scythe' (**falce**) which needs to prepare the 'fodder' (*pabulum* is usually food for animals such as the dragon guarding the fleece which she doped into sleep); *meto* is an agricultural term (to 'mow' or 'reap' giving us *messis* ('harvest')) and Medea is seen as producing the drugs on an industrial scale.

85 Witches in classical texts (e.g. Petronius and Apuleius) are usually described as being able to draw down the moon from the sky – i.e. produce a lunar eclipse. Medea is here only said to 'strive' (**nititur**) to do this but that is enough to indicate her malicious intent, which is the point of the passage. The phrasing is again effective: the moon 'wrestles against her' (**reluctantem** from *luctor*) in its 'running' (**cursu**) as she seeks to 'draw down' (**deducere**) the moon (which is placed for emphasis at the end of the line).

86 Turning day into night (i.e causing a solar eclipse) was another trick of witches: here the phrasing is enhanced by the metaphorical 'horses' of the sun being put away in darkness. The sun was seen as driving a chariot over the skies – famously taken by Phaethon, the son of the sun-god, with disastrous results as told by Ovid in the *Metamorphoses* (2.1–328).

87 Witches often have the power to reverse the course of rivers (cf. Virgil *Aeneid* 4.489) and to stop them flowing at all. Here Hypsipyle keeps the theme of horse-riding from line 86 with the metaphor **refrenat** (she 'reins in' the waters – from *frenum* ('reins of a horse')); **sistit** also indicates making a person or an animal stop moving. **obliqua** means that the rivers 'slope' at an angle and is concessive here: she can stop them even though they have the capacity to swerve at an unlikely angle.

88 Besides causing moving things to stand still, Medea can also cause stationary things to move, and can make forests and rocks shift from their proper place (*loco*). **viva** is interesting: it elsewhere indicates natural rock-formations (e.g. *Metamorphoses* 5.317) but here acts as predicative (she moves them and makes them 'come to life').

89–90 A key part of the witches' arsenal of sympathetic magic was human remains and Medea is skilled at this too: she is content to 'wander' through the tombs suggesting her total ease in the eerie environment, and Ovid gives us the telling visual detail of her dress and hair being untied. Witches seeking to bind another human must not themselves be physically bound in clothing or hair; but the effect is also to suggest a woman who is sexually available (*discinctus* has this sense in *Ars Am.*1.421, Persius 3.31). **tumulos** are 'funeral mounds' made up of earth piled on top of buried corpses or ashes.

90 Witches are said to pull bones out of funeral pyres (**rogis**) once they are cool enough to be touched (hence **tepidis**). The keyword here is **certa** (specific) as this shows that Medea is not just grabbing random bones but knows exactly which parts of the skeleton to choose. The subject matter is grotesque but the line has some pleasing assonance of 'e' and 'o' and is a 'golden line' (two adjectives – verb – two nouns) to form an elegant phrase to match the skill of the witch being described.

91 **simulacra ... cerea:** the 'voodoo' practice of making wax dolls which are then burned or else pierced with pins is well attested in the ancient world (Plato *Laws* 933b, Theocritus 2, Virgil *Eclogue* 8) and Ovid elsewhere (*Amores* 3.7) speculates whether this is the reason for his own sudden impotence. **devovet** means 'she curses' (cf. 164) and **absentes** is an adjectival noun: 'absent people'. **figit** means the same as *defigit*: 'binds with a spell'. Many examples of *defixiones* have been unearthed from the ancient world showing this sort of sympathetic magic. The two verbs neatly frame the line with strong actions of cursing and binding.

92 The detail is vivid: **urget** applies the required pressure and **tenues** (accusative plural) shows that the needles are thin (and sharp). The mention of the **iecur** ('liver') is significant: the liver was the organ most often examined in the form of divination of the future called extispicy (where the priest examined the inner organs of sacrificial victims), but it was also regarded as the centre of human emotions – especially grief and anger – and so possibly the purpose here is to disable the target's anger and force them to set aside their distaste for the person using the love-charm. *miserum* is interesting: taken simply it means 'wretched' and so denotes the unfortunate recipient of this sort of psychological sabotage, but it also denotes 'love-sick' and may be predicative of the state which the person enters once the magic has been applied.

93–4 **melius:** 'I would be better off not to know the rest' implies that there are even more disgusting and perverse practices which she prefers not to know about – this form of *recusatio* hints at more than it delivers. The potential use of the perfect subjunctive shows a feigned modesty here coming from a lady of rank. She then goes on the attack: love ought to be won (**conciliandus**) by fair means – good looks and behaving well – and it is cheating to use these sort of performance-enhancing drugs. *moribus et forma* reverse the order of *facie meritisque* in line 83.

95–6 After the devastating catalogue of Medea's skills described in the third person, Hypsipyle turns to Jason again in the second person singular with a blunt: 'how can you sleep in the same room as this woman?' The key words here are: **amplecti** (to embrace her) indicates the intimacy which would involve letting his guard down, and **uno** ('in one room' – rather than retiring to your own room and locking your door). **somno . . . frui** means more than just 'to sleep' but rather to sleep peacefully and without anxiety (**impavidus**). The point of *nocte silente* is presumably that there is nobody around to help. There is lurking here the tale of Odysseus and Circe where the hero is invited to sleep with the witch and who initially refuses to let her 'strip him naked' and rob him of his 'strength and manhood' (Homer *Odyssey* 10. 337–44).

97–8 **scilicet** introduces a further point for which the speaker has no evidence: '[I don't know but] I suppose . . .'. It was Jason who (as Hypsipyle has already said (cf. 10n.)) made the fire-breathing bulls bear the yoke – but Medea apparently protected him from the flames they emitted and Hypsipyle is anxious to make a rhetorical point: **iugum ferre** is often used of 'bearing the yoke' of marriage and is thus used normally of a wife (cf. Catullus 68.118, Horace *Odes* 2.5.1) and so we have a nice caricature of Jason 'bearing the yoke'; similarly the 'fierce snakes' refer to the dragon which guarded the fleece and which Medea doped into slumber: here again Jason is imagined being drugged in the same way as his prey. There was of course only one dragon, but Hypsipyle clearly thinks that Medea does this sort of thing for a living and so will have drugged a plurality of dragons in her time. For the application of legend to the personal lives of the heroes cf. Scylla's comparison of Minos to the bull with which his wife Pasiphae mated in preference to her husband in *Metamorphoses* 8.136–7. **ut . . . ita** are 'correlatives' and mean 'just as the bulls, so also you.' **ope** comes from *ops* and agrees with *qua* at the start of the line in an instrumental ablative ('with the [same] power with which'). The juxtaposition with **mulcet** is well chosen for oxymoronic effect as the verb indicates 'caressing' and 'soothing' while the noun is one of hard power.

99–100 For **adde** cf. 73n. She demands (**iubet**) that she be 'written up' (**ascribi**) among the 'deeds' (**factis**) of the *proceres* ('great men' – i.e. the Argonauts) and Jason (**tuis** acts in the same role as a genitive pronoun *tui*). The theme of 'writing' is continued with the word **titulo**, which refers to a commemorative plaque or inscription recording events and which also denotes the 'glory' that is Jason's. Hypsipyle at this point seems to concede that Jason and Medea are husband and wife – note the effective juxtaposition of **coniugis uxor** as Medea upstages her 'husband' in a deliberate act of sabotage: **obest** is a powerful verb to end the sentence, denoting her determination to damage the man's reputation by claiming the credit and thus making him look like a stooge in the hands of a more powerful woman.

The intervening lines conclude with telling Jason of the birth of their twins: Hypsipyle considered sending them to their father to plead for his return, but decided against this out of fear of Jason's new partner – their stepmother Medea. This passage owes a lot to Euripides' play 'Medea' in which the children are sent with the fatal wedding-gifts to Jason's new bride.

127–8 The couplet is a powerful tricolon crescendo, with anaphora of Medea in three different cases in the two lines as Hypsipyle rants at her rival with repeated venom. Medea is now the twins' stepmother (**noverca**): the term *noverca* had many pejorative associations so that *novercalis* came to mean 'murderous' and *novercae* were proverbially skilled with poisons: here the word is poised for effect at the end of the line.

128 Medea's hands are 'fitted for any crime': the idiom of *facio ad* is common in Ovid but not often seen elsewhere. Notice the way Hypsipyle escalates Medea's guilt from being 'more than a stepmother' to being a criminal.

129 According to the legend, Medea slowed down the pursuit of her furious family from Colchis by throwing overboard the dismembered body of her brother Apsyrtus as they sailed away: in Ovid's version she is said to have thrown the body-parts over the fields (**agros**). The language is highly expressive: the single brother produces a plurality of 'bodies' – i.e. body-parts – and the word **corpora** is placed in enjambement where we expect a word like *membra* ('limbs'). These are 'torn asunder' (**lacerata**) and then 'scattered' (**spargere**).

130 pignus means a 'pledge' of love or affection and so came to signify the children which could be seen as this (cf. *Heroides* IV.120). The word is ambiguous here as Hypsipyle would have been sending the children as both metaphorical 'pledges of their love' (i.e. children) but also more literally as pledges – 'hostages' or 'stakes' – to ensure his return. The impossibility of a good result is stressed by the juxtaposition of **illa meis** at the end of the line – '*she* would not spare *my*'.

131 Jason has been bewitched, argues Hypsipyle, 'led astray by Colchian poisons' and so is now **demens** or 'out of his mind'. *aufero* can have the meaning 'to lead astray, disturb the judgement of' and also has the more literal sense lurking in that Jason has been 'taken' over the sea and away from her.

132 **diceris** is stressed in enjambement and has the strong sense that 'this is what people say of you', implying that Jason is the object of gossip: it also expresses her disbelief that what is 'said' could be true. **Hypsipyles** is genitive case, and **praeposuisse** is the perfect infinitive of *praepono* in an indirect statement construction ('you are said to have preferred this woman to the bed of Hypsipyle').

133–6 Hypsipyle contrasts herself favourably with Medea in a series of three strong balanced sentences forming a tricolon decrescendo: the first takes up a whole couplet (133–4), the second a single hexameter (135) and the last one a shorter pentameter (136). The three verbs describing Medea are strongly active and pejorative – sexual misconduct (**turpiter cognovit**), betrayal (**prodidit**) and desertion (**deseruit**) – whereas two of the three verbs describing Hypsipyle's actions do not give her any personal agency (the 'torch' gave her in marriage and Lemnos 'holds' her): her only significant action was her virtuous decision to snatch her father from death (**rapui**).

133 The pejorative terms come thick and fast: the line starts with a strong adverb of disapproval (**turpiter** ('disgustingly' or 'shamefully')) and ends with the wonderful oxymoron **adultera virgo** ('virginal adulteress') to show both Medea's innocent appearance and also her immoral intent. **cognovit** means 'had carnal knowledge of' as in line 43 and is a coy euphemism, while **virum** here has the sense 'my husband' and gives more significance to *adultera*.

134 Hypsipyle by contrast does everything by the book: she was married properly and the relationship was one of mutual and

reciprocal commitment. The pairs of balanced pronouns (**me tibi teque mihi**) nicely mirror the mutuality of the love as each appears in each of the two cases: **taeda** means 'torch' and was regarded as a symbol of the ritual wedding at which torches were lit (see 42n.). The torch 'gave' them to each other – a nice way of putting the legal and religious ceremony at the heart of their marriage – and the torch was 'chaste' (**pudica**) to show that Hypsipyle was no *adultera* like her rival.

135 Hypsipyle saved her father Thoas from slaughter when all the men on the island were being slain by the women: this is neatly contrasted with Medea's betrayal of her father (Aeetes, whose Golden Fleece she helped Jason to take). The two phrases are effectively symmetrical, with the verb at the beginning and 'father' at the end of each. Hypsipyle names her own dear father Thoas, whereas Medea's father is left anonymous.

136 Another well-balanced line: verb – a place – me – my – a place – verb. The verb **habet** in the sense of 'has me for an inhabitant' is not common (cf. *Ars Am.* 2.471) and is calculated to suggest that Hypsipyle is doing exactly as she ought; it may also hint to Ovid's readers who knew Euripides' (now lost) play *Hypsipyle* that she was later expelled from Lemnos.

137 **quid refert**: 'What does it matter, if a wicked woman defeats a good one?' Hypsipyle expresses moral outrage as despair: if such things are allowed to happen then why be good? The juxtaposition of **scelerata piam** is effective to show the contrast and the conflict of the two women in stark moral terms.

138 The line is eloquent: Medea with one and the same crime (**ipso crimine**) both got herself a dowry (**dotata est** is perfect passive from

doto) and also 'won' herself a husband. She is presumably thinking of the fleece which she procured for Jason and which acted as her bridal dowry – a gift of money or property paid to the bridegroom usually by the father of the bride and in this case provided unwittingly by the bride's father Aeetes.

139–40 **facinus:** the 'crime' of the Lemnian women was to murder their husbands for replacing them with Thracian mistresses (see 53n.): Hypsipyle – now that she has been supplanted by a mistress – can understand now how they committed this act (**non miror**) although she regards it as immoral (**culpo**): even cowardly women can be stung into violent action by that sort of pain. Hypsipyle's point is to introduce the theme of the final section of the poem (141–64) in which she envisages revenge on Medea and (to a lesser extent) Jason. **quamlibet** is to be taken with **ignavis** – 'however cowardly they are' (cf. 7n.): note the nice personification of *dolor* which 'gives' arms to the women.

141–6 Hypsipyle uses both colloquial language (the peremptory *dic age*, 'go on, tell me') and a long series of unfulfilled conditionals before launching her pair of rhetorical questions, each of them taking up a line of the couplet.

141 Hypsipyle tells him how he ought to have behaved (**ut** meaning simply 'as' and **oportuit** from the impersonal verb *oportet*). There is a nice irony in that she envisages Jason being driven to her shores by 'unfavourable winds', but the word **iniquis** carries overtones of 'unfriendly' or 'treacherous' and suggests that the winds would have done so out of spite against him.

142 Hypsipyle calls Medea simply 'your companion' in haughty disdain, and she is happy to point out that the port belongs to her

(*meos*). **intrasses** is a syncopated form of *intravisses* (cf. *adolesse* in 11, *servasse* in 13). The line has a pleasing euphony in -*tus tuque -mesque meos*, suggestive of the queen rising to fresh rhetorical heights.

143 Hypsipyle has told Jason of his new children in lines 119–24. She now pictures the scene of her coming out of the palace flanked by her two babies. **fetu comitante gemello** forms an ablative absolute construction and the lengthy phrase gives us an impressive picture of Hypsipyle with her twins filling the scene.

144 Jason would have been overcome with embarrassment: the phrase (literally: 'surely the earth would have needed to be asked to open up for you') means 'you would have prayed for the earth to open up'. The phrase goes back to Homer (*Iliad* 4.182, 8.150) and is also found in Virgil (*Aeneid* 4.24). **nempe** introduces a sardonic remark: Jason would have been mortally embarrassed then, even if he was not embarrassed to have left her in the first place. The construction of **roganda fuit** is gerundive + past tense (indicating what would have had to happen).

145–6 The pair of rhetorical questions form a tricolon crescendo with anaphora of *quo . . . quo . . . qua*. The word **vultus** usually means 'face' and here means: 'with what expression would you look at me', i.e. 'would you not be too embarrassed to look me in the eye?' (cf. Sophocles *Oedipus Tyrannus* 1385). **videres** is imperfect subjunctive and so ought to mean 'would you now be looking' which gives her language an immediacy which she escalates further with the indicative *eras* in 146. **scelerate** reminds us of *scelerata* applied to Medea in 137: they are clearly a well-matched pair.

146 The construction is: 'you were (**eras**) worthy (**dignus**) of what sort of (**qua**) death (**nece**) as the reward (**pretio**: predicative dative)

for your treachery (**perfidiae**)?' She starts the question with the powerfully alliterative *perfidiae pretio* and then introduces the idea of a death-sentence (*nece*); she heightens the reality of this by the sudden use of the indicative (*eras* – you were in fact deserving of death) only to reprieve him in the following lines.

147–149 Hypsipyle draws a sharp contrast between her gentle treatment of Jason on the one hand (**quidem**) and her bloody vengeance on Medea.

147 Hypsipyle would not have punished Jason: this is important as her former lover is still important to her and she would (after all) like him to return. The two juxtaposed adjectives **tutus sospesque** both mean 'safe' and when followed by **fuisses** create a good deal of soothing sibilance. **per me** means 'as far as I am concerned' and also hints at the power which Hypsipyle has over him.

148 **dignus** is picked up from 147: Jason deserved to die, and does not now deserve to be 'safe'. The two personal pronouns **tu** and **ego** are used to heighten the contrast between them as well as suggestively putting them into the same line. Hypsipyle describes herself as 'gentle' (**mitis**) at the end of this line, a judgement which the following vengeful lines will explode in some style.

149 The jilted lover Hypsipyle does not name her rival but threatens violence to her simply because she is a *paelicis*. **vultus** here again means 'eyes, gaze' (cf. 145) rather than 'face' as Hypsipyle relishes 'seeing' Medea's blood spilt, but the literal meaning is also present: 'I would have filled my face with the mistress' blood'. **implessem** (from *impleo*) suggests gluttonous enjoyment of the blood in almost cannibalistic frenzy (for which cf. Hecuba's wish to eat the liver of Achilles at Homer *Iliad* 24.212–3).

150 **quosque** picks up *vultus* in the sense of 'eyes' and adds that Jason would also have to watch this spectacle: 'and the eyes which she robbed from me by her poisons – your own [eyes]'. For her comforting thought that Jason was led astray by foul play rather than by his own spontaneous affection for the superior qualities of Medea cf. 83–4, 93–4, 131. The eyes are often regarded as the medium and the object of love in ancient poetry: cf. Propertius 1.1.1, Euripides *Hippolytus* 525–6. The pronominal adjective *tuos* is left to the end of the line for effect, provoking Jason's attention with a sharp comment.

151 'I would be a Medea to Medea' is brilliant: the polyptoton (of the word repeated in different cases), the juxtaposition of the words and above all the use of the name as an ironic threat to the bearer of that name – all this in a short three-word phrase. Medea was renowned as a witch and sorceress and so her name could stand for her qualities: the irony is that Hypsipyle could thus be a metaphorical 'Medea' to (the real) Medea. **forem** is the common alternative form of *essem* (imperfect subjunctive of *sum*).

151–2 Hypsipyle is going to make a prayer in lines 153–4 and prefaces this with saying 'if Jupiter from on high (**ab alto**) is present to my prayers at all (**si … quid**)' – i.e. 'if there is any justice in the world, then …' Jupiter is seen as being 'just' and hence the guardian of justice.

153–64 Hypsipyle's lengthy and detailed curse on Medea is highly charged and revealing of her own suffering (*gemit … destituor … orba … fraudata*) as well as her anger.

153 **quod** is going to pick up the verb *maereat* in 154: 'may she mourn for [the same things for which] Hypsipyle groans'. The point of the line is the parallel suffering of the two women: 'what Hypsipyle groans for, may the wedding-stealer also weep for'. **subnuba** occurs nowhere

else and was coined possibly by the poet himself (on the model of *pronuba* (43: a 'sponsor') and *innuba* (an unmarried girl)) to mean 'an underminer of marriage' or a 'remover of brides'. The 'bed' (**lecti**) stands for the marriage itself by synecdoche.

154 **leges**: 'May she feel the force of her own powers'. *lex* usually means a 'law', but here stands for the exercise of power over others and continues the theme of Hypsipyle treating Medea as she had been treated by her. **ipsa suas** is often juxtaposed for effect. **maereat** and **sentiat** are the first two of a sequence of ten verbs in the optative form of the subjunctive ('would that …').

155–6 Hypsipyle's words are strongly reminiscent of Euripides' *Medea* in which the heroine is abandoned with two sons by Jason. The pathos escalates as Hypsipyle is first 'abandoned as a wife' and then as a 'mother of' (not one but) 'two' [children]. **orba** + ablative means 'widowed' or 'bereft' and in Euripides' play Medea was not 'widowed' as she does not kill Jason but leaves him alive to mourn the deaths of his new bride and his children. Hypsipyle and Medea each have two sons (**totidem natis**).

157 The construction is: 'let her not hold onto her ill-gotten gains for long but let her leave them behind more miserably'. **parta** (perfect participle passive from *pario*, which originally means 'to give birth to') suggests 'offspring' as well as 'gains' and hints at the loss of her children to come, following nicely after lines 155–6. *relinquo* means 'leave behind' and the sense here is that Hypsipyle has lost Jason and so wishes that Medea should also lose her 'gains' with even more misery than Hypsipyle suffered. **peius** is the comparative adverb from *malus*.

158 The line is nicely framed by words of exile (**exulet … fugam**) and the desperation being wished for is well brought out by the universal

toto in orbe as well as the effective verb **quaerat** ('let her seek [and not find]').

159–60 May Medea's future family be as horrible as her original family: may she treat her new relatives as badly as she treated the old ones. Medea famously betrayed her father and murdered her brother: those familiar with Euripides' play will know that she goes on to murder her children when she is betrayed by Jason. The sentence is built around the correlatives **quam . . . tam** . . . ('as . . . so . . .') and the single phrase pairing father and brother in 159 is broken into two separate wishes in 160 with repetition of *tam* for rhetorical effect. The close relationships are brought out by juxtaposition of **fratri germana . . . parenti/ filia**, where the effect is enhanced by the enjambement. The word **acerba** effectively represents the souring of Medea's future family. **viro** ends the line well – Jason will be her husband, and much good may it do her.

161 This sentence continues the theme of 158 with an exploration of the mode and the result of her exile. *consumpserit* ('exhaust [the possibilities of]' from *consumo*) is a striking metaphor for Medea's restless and endless wandering. Her 'trying the sky' is a reference to her flight from Corinth on the chariot of the sun-god at the end of Euripides' play.

162 The catalogue of adjectival descriptors is eloquent and pitiless and is reminiscent of an earlier version of the tale by Accius (where she is *exul inter hostes, exspes, expers desertus vagus*) and more generally of 'curse-language' such as Sophocles *Antigone* 29–30, Euripides *Hippolytus* 1028–31. 'Bloody with her own bloodshed' does not make it clear whose blood she has spilt and readers will think at once of the murdered children: Hypsipyle is only concerned with having Medea end up disgraced by her criminal actions.

163 **Thoantias:** this line is Hypsipyle 'signing' her curse on Medea in formal style with her patronymic title ('daughter of Thoas') and a personal pronoun *ego*. **coniugio fraudata** means 'cheated out of my marriage' and confirms yet again (cf. 5, 17, 20, 22, 41–4, 60, 81) that Hypsipyle regarded herself as legally wedded to Jason.

164 As in line 100, Hypsipyle concedes that Jason and Medea are married as 'bride and husband' (*nuptaque virque* with the repeated *-que* enhancing the pairing of the people), but the compliment to their maritality is undermined by their being verbally enveloped in an 'accursed bed' and by the heavy sarcasm of *vivite* ('have a nice life!' as in Catullus 11.17). Her curse will come true when we turn to poem XII in this collection and hear Medea lament the faithlessness of Jason.

Heroides X

Ariadne was a princess of Crete. Every nine years fourteen young Athenian men and women were sacrificed to the Minotaur – a monster which was half-man, half-bull produced by the sexual union between a bull and the queen Pasiphae, whose husband Minos was the king of Crete and Ariadne's father. Theseus came to Crete to stop this barbaric practice by killing the Minotaur in his labyrinth – a maze of impenetrable complexity built by the legendary craftsman Daedalus. Killing the monster was difficult, but harder still was finding his way out and here Ariadne, who had fallen in love with him, had come to his aid by giving him a ball of wool with which he could retrace his steps. They fled together, with Ariadne (like Medea in poem VI) leaving behind her family and her home to follow her lover, only for him to abandon her on the island of Naxos. In other versions of the tale (such as Catullus 64) she was seen there and rescued by the god Dionysus.

1 The speaker only indicates who is being addressed in 3: the first couplet could have been said by many a heroine of these poems. The sentence is to be understood: 'I found every species of wild beast [to be] gentler than you'. Comparing a callous human to savage beasts is not uncommon, but it has more force here as Ariadne is left abandoned on a desert island which may well contain such *ferae*.

2 **non ulli** means 'to no wild beast' picking up the implied *ferae* from *ferarum*. *credita eram* must be past potential (where *eram* is to be understood as *essem*) and is reflexive rather than passive ('I could have entrusted myself to no beast worse than you'). Ovid likes to use the indicative in cases where we might expect the subjunctive for colloquial and vivid effect.

3 **Theseu:** the addressee's name is signposted in the vocative. Note here the assonance of 'i' in *illo . . . tibi litore mitto.* One wonders how this epistle is to be sent from the island: if a ship is to take it then it could after all also take its authoress. The 'shore' in question is that of Dia, usually identified with the island of Naxos.

4 'The sails carried the ship' confirms that the winds were favourable. **unde** has the same force as *ex quo (litore).* Note also the preponderance of 'm' alliteration in 4–5.

5–6 Ariadne puts the blame for the deception on (1) sleep and then (2) Theseus, whom she addresses with spitting monosyllables (**et tu**) as having 'ambushed my sleep'. **male** is hardly necessary with **prodidit** but it enhances her anger; similarly **per facinus** means 'criminally', completing the triad of pejorative terms. *insidior* is to 'lie in ambush' and so **insidiate** has to be the vocative singular of the perfect participle. The verb indicates hostile intent – as of a wolf towards the sheepfold (*Aeneid* 9.59) – and here the target was the 'sleep': i.e. the sleeping woman.

7–8 Ariadne evokes the time (early morning) beautifully: **tempus erat** is a high epic opening found in Ovid and Virgil to begin a description of a scene usually at night or dawn: for the form cf. *luna fuit* in 17 and *mons fuit* in 25. 'The earth was sprinkled with glassy dew' is a poetic way of hinting that she was cold in the early frost, and the pathetic use of the birds 'complaining' (**queruntur**), hidden in the leaves, mirrors the complaint of Ariadne. *tectae fronde* is also effective: Ariadne would not have known they were there were it not for their sounds.

9 **incertum** is adverbial going with *vigilans* and so meaning 'uncertainly awake' – i.e. half-awake. The point is amplified in

somno languida ('sluggish with sleep'), and Ariadne only begins to move with the final word of the line which leads in enjambement into 10.

10 Ariadne refers to Theseus in the third person although this is part of a speech addressed to him (see 3) in the second person. Theseus is the object of **prensuras** (future participle which has the force of purpose – 'in order to hold') and **semisupina** refers to Ariadne as 'half lying down' – a wonderful image of the woman sitting up and reaching out to hold her lover.

11–12 Her shock is well brought out by the short initial sentence, repeated in incredulity at the end of the couplet. **nullus erat** means 'he was not there' but the adjective *nullus* has much greater force than simply *non* and is like Catullus 8.14. ('not at all'). Ariadne's frantic movements here are well brought out by the polysyndeton (*-que . . . -que . . . -que*), the repeated desperate acts (**iterum retempto**, where the verb is an Ovidian coinage meaning 'to try again') and the escalation from sleepy 'hands' in 10 to whole 'arms' (**bracchia**) in 12 moving over the bed.

13 In 9 Ariadne was only half-awake: her fears now 'shook off her sleep'. The line is nicely framed by the two verbs, and the line has a neat balanced structure of: verb – 'fear' – sleep – 'fear' – verb.

14 **viduo**: the bed is 'widowed' in that it has lost the lover – for *viduus* applied to an inanimate object cf. its application to a city in VI.55 – and this mirrors Ariadne's own condition. The speed of her getting up is well conveyed by her 'throwing her limbs' (where *praecipitata sunt* has a 'middle' sense of 'threw myself out of bed' but giving due emphasis to the limbs (*membra*) almost as if they had a mind of their own).

15–16 Two obvious signs of grief for women: beating the breast and tearing the hair. The plosive alliteration of 'p' in 15 enhances the idea of the noise of the beating. *adductus* in 104 means 'hands put together' and that is the sense here: she drew her palms together and used them to make her breast resound.

16 Ovid has a nice thought here: Ariadne had been asleep (**e somno** meaning 'after sleep') and so her hair was untidy (**turbida**) anyway (**ut erat**): so she simply tore at it in rage and grief. For **rupta** in this context of grief cf. VI.27, where it refers to clothing which is 'torn'.

17 **luna fuit:** 'There was a moon' is not simply an indication of time (early morning) and the cold clear night which has passed (there is dew on the ground (7)) but also explains how she could see her way to look for him – her looking expressed in two verbs, *specto* ('look') and *cernam* ('see'), well chosen to show that she could not see what she was looking for. *cernam* is a subjunctive in the conditional clause understood from *specto*: 'I look to see if I might see . . .'. The question raised in 17 is answered in 18 with a sad repetition of the key words (*nil nisi litora . . . nil nisi litus*) and the poignant double negative of **nil nisi**. *videant* here is subjunctive in a final relative clause ('the eyes have nothing <u>to see</u> except shore').

19–20 Ariadne's frantic movements are well shown by the darting **nunc huc nunc illuc** and her scrambled thoughts are also conveyed by the phrase **utroque sine ordine** ('either way at random'). The strong verb **curro** – she is 'running' – is undercut in 20 by the difficulty of running on sand, a difficulty enhanced by her 'girlish' feet which are less athletic (and also more attractive). Note here the rhythm indicative of the slow progress produced by the combination of deep (**alta**) sand and girlish (**puellares**) feet, where the dactyl slows down to a sluggish spondee and the double 'l' sound in *āltă pŭ/ēllār/ēs*. 20 is another golden line, with the central verb framed by the adjectives on one side and the nouns on the other.

21-2 Construe: 'the hollow rocks sent back your name 'Theseus' to [me as I was] shouting all over the shore'. *reddo* is a good verb for 'echo' (cf. *Metamorphoses* 3.361, Lucretius 4.571) as it denotes 'giving back' the sound like a boomerang; and note the pseudo-scientific detail of 'hollow' applied to the surrounding rock-face. **toto litore** suggests that she is indeed running all over the shore (19).

23-4 The echoes are the only sound she hears coming back to her, and Ovid brilliantly evokes this in the inverted repetition of **locus ipse . . . ipse locus.** *quotiens . . . totiens* are correlatives ('as many times as I [called], so many times did . . .'). She sentimentally endows the place with a desire (**volebat**) to bring help to her in her love-sick misery (**miserae**): for the pathetic effect of echoes like this cf. the whole episode of Narcissus and Echo in *Metamorphoses* 3.339-510.

25-6 Ariadne in Catullus (64. 124-31) had gone up to the mountain and then (when she could see nothing from there) had come back down to the shore: Ovid reverses this movement and has her climbing only after her desperate running on the sand. She describes her vantage point in vivid detail and typical Ovidian imagery: the shrubs 'here and there' (**rari**) on the peak 'visible' (**apparent**) from the shore, the rock-face hanging 'eaten away' (**adesus**) by the 'rough' waters of the sea. Ariadne tells us this partly to emphasize her own desperation in climbing such a forbidding rock.

27-8 The difficulty of the climb is mirrored in the long syllables of **ascendo vires** followed by more rapid movement of **animus dabat**. The vast expanse of sea is well evoked in the long phrasing of the golden line 28 (where the first half of the line consists of two nouns to be taken with the two adjectives in the second half after the central verb); and the almost synonymous phrasing of **prospectu metior** ('I survey with looking out') reinforces the idea of long and hard gazing. **alta** ('deep') is assumed from the distance of the watery horizon from the shoreline.

29–30 Ariadne feels the power of the wind from her mountainous vantage point and then catches sight of Theseus' sails (**carbasa**) stretched by the (same) 'headlong' (**praecipiti**) wind. The connection of ideas is inspired: the winds are 'harsh' (**crudelibus**) in a literal sense on her face, and then they are also 'harsh' in taking her lover away from her. Theseus was cruel in leaving her and the winds were 'also' cruel, joining in the conspiracy against her. *carbasus* literally means 'linen' and so comes to mean 'sails' by synecdoche for '[linen] sails'. The speed of the wind (*praecipiti*) mirrors the haste with which Theseus left her.

31 Translate: 'as I saw that which (*quae*) I thought I did not deserve to see'. The language is strained: there is the sense that she cannot believe she has seen the ship sailing away and also the feeling that she does not deserve this sort of treatment. **putarem** is imperfect subjunctive indicating that she 'would not think she had seen this' – if it were not before her eyes.

32 Ariadne returns to her semi-alive state (cf. 9–10 and *languere* in 33) and the mention of 'ice' reminds us of the 'glassy dew' in 7–8. **semianimis** is to be scanned as four syllables by sounding the first 'i' as a consonant: *sēm(i)ănĭm/is*. The effect of this is to enhance the feeling of her stupor.

33 The somnolence of the long syllables in the opening of the line (*nēc lānguēr-*) is effective in maintaining the mood; this is then broken in the quicker pace of the following dactyls. The sudden arousal of

Ariadne is also enhanced by the repetition of **excitor** in epanalepsis from the fifth foot of 33 to the first foot of 34.

34 **summa voce** must mean 'at the top of my voice' and her repeated cries are evoked in the pleonasm of *vōcĕ vŏcō* where the different quantities produce an echo effect.

35 **quo fugis?** might seem to be a silly question but it functions as a rebuke more than a request for information. **exclamo** picks up the idea of 'shouting' from 34. **scelerate** is less harsh ('crook') than (e.g.) *perfide* which is how Catullus has her address him (64.133). The point here is that she clings to the possibility that he has simply forgotten her and that she might get him to come back for her: Catullus (64.58) called Theseus *immemor* and her behaviour in the following lines is that of somebody who thinks he has simply made a mistake of forgetting (*oblitos* 42) rather than a deliberate act of dereliction. When the truth dawns on her later she (78) refers to him as an 'oath-breaker' (*periuri*). **revertere** is the singular imperative from the deponent verb *revertor* and so means 'turn round', a point to be amplified and explained in the following line.

36 'Turn your ship: it does not have its [full] number' – i.e. it does not have the full complement of mariners on board as I am not there with you all. **flecte ratem** will be repeated at the end of the poem (151).

37 Understand **dixi** after **haec ego**: and scan **deerat** as two syllables with the -*ee*- read as a singly diphthong. This, combined with the repetition of sounds in *plangore replebam*, well conveys her wailing lamentation. Her point in **quod voci deerat** ('what was lacking to my voice') is that she filled out (**replebam**) the inevitable gaps in her (otherwise fluent) stream of speech by beating her breast (**plangore**).

38 A lovely play on words ('paronomasia'): the Latin for 'word' (**verba**) is close in sound to the word for 'blows' (**verbera**) and so Ovid can convey the mixed stream of vocal and percussive sounds with the two words in the same half of the line. There is a strong element of irony in this arch account of the performance.

39–40 **audire** means 'to hear' while **cernere** is more generally to 'perceive' (cf. 17n.). 'If you could not hear me, and to make sure that (*ut* + subjunctive as a purpose clause) you could somehow or other (**saltem**) notice me, my hands, thrown around in all directions, made signals'. Notice again (cf. 14) Ovid's use of the 'middle' form of the passive: Ariadne threw her hands around and the repetition of the movement is suggested in the repetition of sounds in *iactatae late*.

41–2 Ariadne makes a makeshift flag to wave at Theseus by putting white clothing on a long stick. **candida** serves several purposes: (1) white clothing would be better at attracting attention; (2) the word hints at the 'white' sails which Theseus later in the legend forgot to put on the mast of this ship causing his aged father Aegeus to think he had died and so commit suicide in grief (see Catullus 64.207–48); and (3) *candida* is the word for 'fair' in the case of a beautiful girl, and so is apt for this fair girl. **scilicet oblitos** is eloquent: she is acting on the assumption (see 35n.) that Theseus had simply forgotten her. **mei** is the genitive singular of the personal pronoun (the verb *obliviscor* takes the genitive case) while **admonitura** is a future participle with final sense ('to remind').

43 So long as she could see the ship she had hope; but now Theseus had been taken from her gaze. The tense of **ereptus eras** is pluperfect, suggesting that the narrative has moved on in time from the previous lines. **tum denique flevi** is emphatic and moving: she has now lost

hope and so finally (**denique**) weeps. The short clauses are also eloquent of her sudden realization of the truth.

44 A line of some subtlety. *torpeo* indicates 'sloth' or 'inactivity', while *gena* here means 'eyes' and *mollis* means 'soft' or 'feminine'. So the line means 'my womanly eyes had been numb with grief beforehand' (*ante* being used adverbially). Ovid is referring to a previous state of shock in which the expression of grief was impossible, and his choice of **genae** (which usually means 'cheeks') rather than *oculi* for eyes is presumably to hint at the entire face paralysed with shock rather than simply an inability to cry.

45 **quid potius facerent:** 'what else could they do?' is a nice way of saying: (1) I could not restrain my tears and (2) I had run out of any other options now that the ship was no longer visible (46). The lamentation is well conveyed in the juxtaposed repetition of *me mea*. **lumina** ('lights') means 'eyes' here, as often in poetry.

46 **vela:** Ariadne says 'your sails' in effective synecdoche for 'your ship' as it would be the sails which would be most visible on a distant ship and as the sails were carrying him away from her. The final pronominal adjective **tua** is sad and effective, as is the plangent alliteration of 'v'.

47–50 Ariadne expresses her grief either in manic movement or in catatonic stillness. This is psychologically convincing and shows Ovid's interest in human behaviour.

47 **diffusis . . . capillis** are to be taken together in a descriptive ablative absolute phrase – 'with my hair streaming' – but this is not simply repeating 16 where her hair was untidy from sleep. The point of *diffusis* (from *diffundo*) is that her hair streamed behind her as she

moved quickly: **erravi** indicates random movement (cf. 6.162) and **sola** ('alone') is of course pathetic.

48 **Ogygio:** *Ogygius* means 'Theban' because Ogygos was a founder and early king of Thebes: Bacchus (Dionysus) came from Thebes and so he can be described as Ogygian. Ogygia is also the name of the island home of Calypso – the solitary nymph left by Odysseus in Homer *Odyssey* V – and it is faintly possible that Ovid is here choosing the recondite term for 'Theban' to recall the tale of Calypso. A 'Bacchant' (**Baccha**) was a woman worshipper of Bacchus and was also a byword for mad raving behaviour – indeed the alternative term for Bacchant – 'maenad' – also means 'mad woman' in Greek (cf. Homer *Iliad* 22.460). Bacchus is of course highly relevant in this legend as in most accounts the god comes to Dia (Naxos) and rescues Ariadne from her plight.

49–50 After the manic movement, the cold still depression. Ariadne was still 'gazing out to sea' as before but here she is doing so 'cold', as much like a stone as the stone on which she sits. For the image of a stone as a metaphor for total lack of feeling cf. Homer *Iliad* 16.35–6. The repetition of phrasing using the correlatives **quam ... lapis ...,** **tam lapis ...** brings out the glassy catatonic state she is in.

51–2 **torum:** the *torus* must be the makeshift 'bed' which they had used the night before. The point is that this bed now showed no evidence of its former occupants: it had welcomed them the night before, but now was 'not going to bring forward [evidence of] their having been received'. Ariadne brings out the confusion in her mind with the repetition: the bed *acceperat* them but now they were not visibly **acceptos.** Is she going mad? Yes!

53–4 The meaning is: 'I touch your 'imprints' – which is all I can touch – in place of [touching] you'. The **vestigia** are the indentations of

Theseus' body on the couch; and the **strata** (perfect participle passive from *sterno* and so meaning 'things strewn') are the bedclothes which 'grew warm by your limbs'. Ariadne's longing for Theseus is well conveyed by the polyptoton of **tua . . . te . . . tuis.**

55–8 Ariadne now addresses the bed directly: not only because she has no other part of Theseus to address apart from his former bed but also because it represents the intimacy which they so recently shared.

55 **lacrimis . . . profusis** is to be taken after **toro manante** so that the double ablative phrase means: 'as the bed was soaked by my tears poured forth'. Once again there is emphasis on the physical expression of Ariadne's grief through her copious tears: cf. 43 and contrast her *frigida* state in 49. The word order enhances this with the juxtaposition of the tears and the bed in the line as in life and the accumulative force of the two 'liquid' words *manante profusis*.

56 'The two of us have pressed upon you – give back the two of us' recalls Ariadne's rebuke at 36 and looks forward to a similar repetition of *ambo* in 57.

57 **ambo** occurs just before the caesura and at the end of the line, with a rhetorical question of indignant disbelief.

58 Ariadne turns her venom on the bed for the offences of its occupant; 'traitor' (**perfide**) is more appropriate to Theseus and it is he who is her 'better half' (literally 'the greater part of me'). **lectule** is an affectionate diminutive from *lectus* and the inconsistency between her calling it 'traitor' and her affection is mirrored by her strong expression of love (**pars maior**) for the man who cheated her. Her pathetic question ('where is he?') reminds us of her question to him at 35.

59 Ariadne now gives fuller rein to her feelings in a tirade of rhetorical questions and plaintive descriptions of her isolation. The subjunctives **faciam** and **ferar** are both deliberative: 'what am I do to and where am I to travel all alone?' The verbs could be future indicatives, but her description of her hopeless situation in the following lines makes it clear that her mood is one expecting the answer 'there is nothing I can do'. **vacat cultu** tells us that the island is empty and devoid of 'habitation/cultivation' – *cultus* being derived from *colo* which means to 'inhabit' and also to 'cultivate' – as explained in the next line.

60 'the works of men and cattle' is a good way of saying 'signs of human agriculture' and borrowed from Homer (*Odyssey* 10.98). The reader has to understand it as: *non hominum [facta] video, non ego [video] facta boum*. Without human help she will not be able to find transport (see 61) to where Theseus has gone and may well starve to death without food.

61 **mare** is the subject of the sentence: 'the sea girds every side of the land' and yet there is 'nowhere a sailor'. The line uses emphatic alliteration of 'n' and is nicely framed by the words *omne . . . nusquam/nulla* showing the totality of the sea and the total lack of mariners. One might expect that an island would produce ships and sailors – but not this one.

62 **puppis:** there is no 'poop' (standing by synecdoche for 'ship') to make its way (the future participle **itura** again having predicative function) through the dubious ways. The phrase **ambiguas vias** sardonically reminds us of the way Ariadne had helped Theseus through the very 'dubious ways' of the Labyrinth in Crete and now needs this sort of help herself.

63 No sooner has Ariadne lamented the lack of a ship than she now dismisses the idea: **finge dari ... ratemque** means 'imagine

companions, the winds and the ship are given to me': the list of items is neatly joined with polysyndetic repetition of *-que* as if she is counting them off on her fingers. Her purpose is not to cheer herself up ('I am fine without them') but the opposite ('no amount of help can help me now').

64 Ariadne has burned her bridges in every way in pinning her hopes on Theseus and in the process betraying her family. In the manner of a catechism she asks a question and then answers it for herself. **sequar** is again deliberative subjunctive and means here 'what am I to make for?' Her **terra paterna** ('land of my fathers') is Crete which now 'denies her any approach' after her complicity in the death of her half-brother the Minotaur.

65–6 **ut** in both lines here is concessive: 'even though ... I will still be an exile'. The imagined ease of the voyage is well conveyed in the juxtaposition of *felici pacata* and then the choice of the verb **labar** ('glide'). Aeolus was the god of the winds who famously controlled the winds to allow Odysseus to travel homewards in Homer *Odyssey* 10. Ariadne's point is that a passport to anywhere is useless when she, as an exile, has nowhere she can land, her lament enhanced by the assonance of 'e' here.

67–9 **aspiciam** is a strong future indicative and Ariadne ironically juxtaposes **ego te** to underline her regret that she will not in fact see Crete again, with the sorrow enhanced by the mournful repetition of sounds in *te Crete centum*. The island of Crete is described in three interesting phrases in three successive lines. The massive size and advanced urban civilization of the island is suggested by its being 'organized into a hundred cities' (surely a place so civilized and so big could have room for her?) It was also the land 'known to Jupiter as a boy', as the infant god was hidden from his father Kronos in a cave on

Mount Dicte in Crete when his father was seeking to kill all his children to prevent one of them from overthrowing him. Jupiter is invoked elsewhere (VI.152) as a symbol of justice and the line perhaps hints that the god will not stand by and see such treachery go unpunished – a point amplified in the next line.

69 **parenti:** Crete is lastly said to be a land 'ruled over by my righteous parent' – a reference to the legendary King Minos whose reputation for justice gave him the role of judge of the dead in Virgil's underworld (*Aeneid* 6.432–3). *regnata* is passive and *parenti* is a dative of agent ('ruled by my father'), the harsh severity of the justice being brought out by the juxtaposition of *iusto regnata*. Minos is both Ariadne's father and also the just ruler of her homeland; both the man and the land are 'dear' to her and both have been 'betrayed' (**prodita sunt**) by her actions to be explained in the following lines.

71–2 Theseus defeated the Minotaur and so was 'victorious' (**victor**): Ariadne's crime was to stop him from dying in the Labyrinth (here referred to as the 'winding building' (**tecto . . . recurvo**)) by giving him threads (**fila**) to lead him out (**pro duce:** literally 'taking the role of leader'). **regerent** is a subjunctive in a final relative clause: 'threads to guide your footsteps'. The long sequence of 're' sounds in *morerere rec-* is suggestive of the winding paths of the maze. Ariadne was complicit in the murder of the Minotaur by supplying the getaway for the murderer.

73–4 Theseus had promised eternal love, much as Jason did in VI.60, and the imperfect tense of **dicebas** suggests that this was something he did on a regular basis to reassure her. The translation is: 'by the dangers themselves, I swear that you will be mine so long as either of us is alive'. The point of swearing by the 'dangers' (*pericula*) is that he risks death during the ordeal if he is found to be swearing falsely; and the placing of the personal pronoun *ego* in the middle of the oath adds emphasis

to his personal commitment and risk. There is also pleasing anaphora
here of **per . . . pericula-.** *fore* is the shortened form of *futuram esse* and
note that 74 is framed by 'you' (*te*) and 'me' (*meam*).

75–6 After the rhetoric of Theseus' oath, Ariadne spells out the plain
truth: she is not his even though both of them are still alive – if (that is,
she adds tartly) one can be said to be alive who is already dead thanks to
the treachery of her 'man'. 75 is neatly framed by **vivimus . . . vivit**. 76
runs on from 75 in enjambement and is a wonderful epitaph for Ariadne,
summing up her fate and her plight in stark sexist terms with **femina**
and **viri** framing the line. She is a <u>woman</u> 'buried' by the deceit of a
treacherous <u>man</u>: note also the juxtaposition of the two 'deceit' words
periuri fraude for added emphasis and the alliteration of 'v' and 'f'.

119–24 Ariadne fears dying without her mother, and then widens the
lament to her realization that she will die all alone and remain
unburied, a fate much feared in the ancient world with the attendant
belief that the soul would not pass safely to the Underworld if the
body was not properly buried.

119 **moritura** is the future participle of *morior* and means 'on the
point of death'.

120 **condat** is another final subjunctive after *qui*: 'nor will there be
[someone] to close my eyes with his fingers'. *lumina* ('lights')
commonly means 'eyes' (cf. 45) but here it has a flavour of its deeper
meaning alongside *condat* with the sense of 'burying' the 'light' as a
synonym for death.

121 The **spiritus** is the last breath exhaled: the juxtaposition of **infelix
peregrinas** gives the phrase explanatory force: 'unfortunate [in that]
foreign are the breezes it will pass into'.

122 Ariadne imagines a proper funeral with her limbs arranged (*positos*) on the bier and a friendly hand will anoint them before the cremation and subsequent burial of the ashes.

123 Leaving an enemy's unburied corpse to be picked by birds is a threatened punishment found in Greek literature (e.g. Sophocles *Antigone* 205–6, *Ajax* 1064–5) and also in Ovid's eloquent curse-poem *Ibis* (169–72). Ariadne thought she was Theseus' beloved – and he is treating her like an enemy. The interweaving of the **ossa ... inhumata** with the **volucres ... marinae** nicely mirrors the birds mangling the bones, and **superstabunt** is both suitably spondaic and maliciously unspecific – they will 'hover' – as if the speaker cannot bring herself to spell out what comes next.

124 **sepulcra** is sarcastic: is this (non-burial) the sort of 'burial' which my dutiful acts (*officiis*) deserve (*digna*)?

125–50 Ariadne now imagines Theseus' triumphant homecoming to Athens and draws a stark contrast between his glory and her humiliation.

125 Cecrops was the founder and early king of Athens – said to have been a serpent below the waist and very much the stuff of legend – and so the 'Cecropian port' is the port of Athens: the name begins the theme of 'legend-making' which the following lines will continue. There is a touch of irony (and plosive 'p' alliteration) in **patria** ('fatherland') as the story often narrates that Theseus had a sad homecoming as his father had committed suicide, convinced of his son's demise (see Catullus 64. 241–8). **receptus** is the perfect participle passive: when you have been 'received in your fatherland'.

126 The line is textually corrupt in the manuscripts but the reading adopted here makes good sense: she imagines Theseus to have 'taken his

stand' 'lofty (**celsus**) in the sight' of his 'crowd'. *os* means 'face' or 'mouth'
and also 'gaze': there may also be the sense that he is high in their 'mouth'
in the sense that he is headline news (cf. *narraris* 127) in Athens.

127 Theseus is the agent of his own myth-making: **narraris** is short
for *narraveris* and is second person singular future perfect indicative
(cf. *steteris* 126) meaning 'when you [will] have told the tale of . . .'. His
foe was both man and bull at the same time: the storyteller has to spell
this out as his audience would not have perhaps understood the term
'Minotaur': it also gives him the chance to use the epic polysyndeton
-que . . . -que.

128 Theseus now goes on to describe the Labyrinth in terms of its
solid structure (**saxea tecta**) and its cunning paths (**dubias vias**). Take
the words thus: 'the halls of rock cut into confusing paths'. The paradox
of a house of paths is pointed out by the juxtaposion of *tecta vias.*

129 **narrato** is a strong future form of the imperative (= 'be sure to
tell') and gives the phrase a more formal and authoritative tone
appropriate to this bitter prayer. **sola** is hypallage (transferred epithet),
as it is Ariadne and not the land which is alone: her isolation is in
bitter contrast to the 'crowd' of Theseus' audience (126). **tellure** is also
ominous – the word often indicates the site of burial – and **relictam**
sums up her plight with one final word.

130 **titulis** refers to the 'record of honours' (cf. VI.100) and is
heavily sarcastic here: Ariadne classes herself as one of his great
achievements. *subripienda* is the gerundive form meaning 'to be
removed'.

131–2 The lines as they stand in the manuscript are almost certainly
misplaced and are to be read between lines 110 and 111.

133–4 Ariadne continues her wishes, with an optative subjunctive ('would that the gods . . .'). *facio* followed by *ut* + subjunctive means 'see to it that . . .'. Ariadne imagines that Theseus saw her from the top of the poop deck and speculates that if he were able to do so, then her sad form would have made him change his expression (**vultus** means 'face' and so 'facial expression'). The emphasis in the couplet is on the outward appearances: if he saw her then he would himself wear a different appearance. **videres** is imperfect subjunctive which in conditional clauses usually refers to the present time ('if you were seeing me now'): as the chance to do this has passed (see 135), the force of the tense is 'if you were still able to see me'.

135 'Look at me with the mind with which you can (see me)' means 'picture how I am now'. **qua** goes with **mente**. The imperative **aspice** is repeated in 137.

136 Understand *me* with the participle **haerentem** ('sticking'). The rock-face is made more vivid by the extra detail of the 'free-moving' (**vaga**) waters battering at it, reminding us of the details given in 26.

137 **demissos . . . capillos:** mourners typically untied their hair and allowed it to hang loose: Ariadne has told us that her hair was untidy from sleep (16) and that it was streaming behind her as she roved like a Bacchant (47), while now it is simply 'let down' like that of one mourning. **more** + genitive means 'in the manner of a . . .'.

138 Ariadne's clothes are wet with tears, as if (**sicut**) they had been soaked with rain: for her copious weeping cf. 55. The line is effectively framed by the **tunicas . . . graves**.

139 A vivid simile, in which her body 'shivers' like crops 'driven' by the North winds. **Aquilo** is the North wind and the choice is well made as

it is both a strong wind capable of acting on a field full of corn and also a cold wind which makes the skin 'shiver'.

140 This line reminds us that – however implausibly – Ariadne is writing a letter as she speaks. The 'letter' wobbles (**labat**) when pressed down by her 'shaking (finger)-joint'. The choice of **pressa** rather than (say) *scripta* makes it clear that she is writing on a wax tablet where pressure would be required to make the marks in the wax.

141–3 Ariadne's 'good service' (**meritum**) to Theseus was to help him escape Crete: she now concedes that has 'ended badly' (**male cessit**) for her (see 103–4) and so claims to be beseeching him not to reward her for her good deeds but not to punish her for them either. **sit** is a iussive subjunctive ('let there be') and **debita** is a strong term here ('you do not owe me any *gratia*') leading to her rhetorical conclusion – you certainly do not owe me any punishment.

143–4 Ariadne spells out the logic of her statement: I may not be the cause of your safety, but there is no reason for you to be the cause of my death. Note the contrasting terms **salutis** and **necis** at the ends of the two lines and the finger-jabbing of the series of monosyllables in 144.

145–6 Translate: 'I, unfortunate one, stretch out (*tendo*) these hands – tired as they are with beating my mournful breasts – over the wide seas'. **plangendo** is the ablative of the gerund from *plango* ('with beating'): for this image cf. 37. 'Mournful' better describes Ariadne herself but she transfers the epithet to her breasts. **trans** is surprising – she cannot literally extend her hands 'across' the seas, but she may be thinking of the work of her hands (the letter which consists of this poem) which will go 'across' the waters.

147 Ariadne repeats the pattern of 145 (*has tibi ... infelix ... tendo ... manus: hos tibi ... ostendo ... maesta capillos*) in a fresh rhetorical assault. 'The hairs which are left me' (**qui superant**) suggest that she has torn out many of them in grief, and there is a pleasing jingle of *tendo ... ostendo*.

148 **lacrimas:** Ariadne has claimed (142) that she is not begging by her just deserts and here claims to be begging by her tears. Her language here changes register – after the high style of the previous lines – into simple and movingly unaffected speech.

149 Ariadne made this command at 36 and now tells him how to do it: turn the sails round (**verso ... velo**) and 'glide back', suggesting that a return voyage will be easy. There is a harsh note of irony in 'change the sails' as Theseus was said to have promised his father Aegeus that he would change the sails on his way home to indicate to him from afar that he had survived the ordeal: he forgot to do this and the old man took his life.

150 If Theseus does this and she has died before he reaches her, then he will at least be able to take her bones to Athens for a decent burial. **occidero** is future perfect indicative followed by a future tense **feres** in a simple conditional clause relating to future time: 'if I will have died [by then], you will take the bones'.

Vocabulary

While there is no Defined Vocabulary List for A-level, words in the OCR Defined Vocabulary List for **AS** are marked with * so that students can quickly see the vocabulary with which they should be particularly familiar.

*a, ab (+ ablative) — away from, by
abeo, abire, abi(v)i — to go away from
absens, absentis — absent
abstraho, abstrahere, abstraxi, abstractum — to draw, drag away
abundo, abundare, abundavi — to overflow
*ac — and
accessus, -ūs, m — admittance
*accipio, accipere, accepi, acceptum — to receive
acerbus -a -um — bitter
acus -ūs, f — pin, needle
*ad (+ accusative) — to, towards
*adde (imperative from addo, addere, addidi) — consider also
adduco, adducere, adduxi, adductum — to draw towards
adedo, adesse, adedi, adesum — to eat away at
admoneo, admonere, admonui, admonitum — to advise, suggest
adolesco, adolescere, adolevi, adultum — to grow to manhood
adoro, adorare, adoravi, adoratum — to beg
adscribo, adscribere, adscripsi, adscriptum — to write up in addition
*adsum, adesse, adfui — to be present
adulter, adultera, adulterum — adulterous
*adversus -a -um — opposing
Aeetes — Aeetes, King of Colchis and father of Medea

Aegeus -i, m	Aegeus (father of Theseus)
Aeolus -i, m	Aeolus (god of the winds)
aequor, aequoris, n	sea
aer, aeris, m	air
aeripes, aeripedis	bronze-hooved
Aesonides, m	son of Aeson, Jason
aestas, aestatis, f	summer
aetas, aetatis, f	age, generation
Aethra, Aethrae, f	Aethra (mother of Theseus)
age (*imperative*)	come now
*ager, agri, m	field, land
*ago, agere, egi, actum	to drive, do, accomplish, spend time
ait	he says, he said
alterno, alternare, alternavi, alternatum	to alternate
*altus -a -um	high, deep
alvus -i, f	womb, belly
ambiguus -a -um	unclear, dubious
ambo -ae, -o	both
*amica -ae, f	female friend
*amor, amoris, m	love
amplector, amplecti, amplexus sum (deponent)	to embrace
*an	or
anguis -is, m	snake
*animus -i, m	mind, spirit
*ante (+ accusative)	before
*appareo, apparere, apparui	to be visible
*aqua, aquae, f	water
aquilo, aquilonis, m	north wind
ardeo, ardere, arsi, arsum	to burn
Argo	the Argo (ship of the Argonauts)
Argolicus -a, -um	belonging to Argos (region of Greece)
Argolis, Argolidos, f	woman of Argos

aries, arietis, m	ram
*arma, armorum, n (plural)	weapons
aro, arare, aravi, aratum	to plough
articulus -i, m	finger-joint
artus -ūs, m (plural)	limbs
*ascendo, ascendere, ascendi, ascensum	to climb up
aspicio, aspicere, aspexi, aspectum	to see, look at
assuetus -a -um	usual, familiar
atque	and
auctor, auctoris, m	parent, originator
*audio, audire, audivi, auditum	to hear
*aufero, auferre, abstuli, ablatum	to carry off
aura -ae, f	breeze
aureus -a -um	golden
auro, aurare, auravi, auratum	to gild, make gold in colour
*aut	or
avis, avis, f	bird

Baccha, Bacchae,	Bacchant (female worshipper of Bacchus)
barbarus -a -um	foreign
*bene	well
*bis	twice
bos, bovis, m	cow
bracchium -ii, n	arm

*cado, cadere, cecidi	to fall
*caedes, caedis, f	slaughter
caerulus -a -um	sky-blue
candidus -a -um	white, bright, pretty
canto, cantare, cantavi, cantatum	to sing
capillus -i, m	hair
carbasa -orum, n (plural)	sails
carina -ae, f	boat
carmen, carminis, n	song, spell

*carus -a -um	dear
*castra, castrorum, n (plural)	camp
castus -a -um	pure, holy, chaste
*causa -ae, f	cause, case
Cecropius -a -um	Athenian
*cedo, cedere, cessi, cessum	to turn out
*celo, celare, celavi, celatum	to hide
celsus -a -um	lofty, high
*centum	100
cereus, cerea, cereum	waxen
*cerno, cernere, crevi, cretum	to see, discern
*certus -a -um	sure, specific
cesso, cessare, cessavi, cessatum	to cease, to be slack in performing
*ceterus -a -um	the rest
*cingo, cingere, cinxi, cinctum	to surround, encircle
circumspicio, circumspicere, circumspexi, circumspectum	to look around at
civilis, civile	civil, internecine
*clamo, clamare, clamavi, clamatum	to shout
*coepi, coepisse, coeptum	to begin
*cognosco, cognoscere, cognovi, cognitum	to get to know, find out
*cogo, cogere, coegi, coactum	to compel, drive together
Colchus -a -um	coming from Colchis, Colchian
colligo, colligere, collegi, collectum	to gather together
coma -ae, f	hair
*comes, comitis, m or f	companion
comitor, comitari, comitatus sum (deponent)	to accompany
concavus -a -um	hollow
concido, concidere, concidi	to fall down
concieo, conciere, concivi, concitum	to stir, urge, rouse
concilio, conciliare, conciliavi, conciliatum	to win over, procure
*condo, condere, condidi, conditum	to close, hide

coniugium -i, n	marriage
*coniunx, coniugis, m or f	spouse
conscendo, conscendere, conscendi, conscensum	to climb
*consumo, consumere, consumpsi, consumptum	to consume, use, devour
conterreo, conterrere, conterrui, conterritum	to terrify
conubialis, -e	marital
cor, cordis, n	heart
*corpus, corporis, n	body
*credo, credere, credidi, creditum	to believe, trust
credulus -a -um	believing, credulous
Crete, -es	the island of Crete
*crimen, criminis, n	crime, charge
*crudelis -e,	cruel
cruentus -a -um,	bloody
culpo, culpare, culpavi, culpatum	to blame
cultus -ūs, m	appearance, dress
*cum	when, since, although
*cupidus -a -um	desirous
*cupio, cupere, cupi(v)i, cupitum	to desire
*cur	why
*curro, currere, cucurri, cursum	to run
cursus -ūs, m	running, course
damnum -i, n	loss
*de (+ ablative)	about, down from
*debeo, debere, debui, debitum	to owe, must
deduco, deducere, deduxi, deductum	to draw down
demens, dementis	mad, foolish
demitto, demittere, demisi, demissum	to send down
*denique	finally, at length
dens, dentis, m	tooth
desero, deserere, deserui, desertum	to desert, abandon
*desino, desinere, desivi, desitum	to leave off, cease

destituo, destituere, destitui, destitutum	to abandon, desert
desum, deesse, defui	to be lacking
detego, detegere, detexi, detectum	to uncover
*deus -i, m	god
devinco, devincere, devici, devictum	to defeat
devoveo, devovere, devovi, devotum	to curse
*dextra -ae, f	right hand
*dico, dicere, dixi, dictum	to say, speak
diffundo, diffundere, diffudi, diffusum	to dishevel (hair), to pour out
digero, digerere, digessi, digestum	to arrange
digitus -i, m	finger
*dignus -a -um	worthy, deserving
*dirus -a -um	terrible, dread
*discedo, discedere, discessi, discessum	to depart
discingo, discingere, discinxi, discinctum	to untie the clothing, ungird
*diu	for a long time
diurnus -a -um	lasting one day
*dives, divitis	rich
*do, dare, dedi, datum	to give
*dolet (impersonal verb)	it pains me
*dolor, doloris, m	pain, grief
*donum -i, n	gift
doto, dotare, dotavi, dotatum	to provide a dowry
draco, draconis, m	snake
*dubius -a -um	doubtful, dubious
*dum	while, until
duo	two
*dux, ducis, m	leader
*e (+ ablative)	from out of
*egeo, egere, egui	to want, lack
*ego, me, mei, me	I (first person pronoun)

emereo, emerere, emerui, emeritum	to earn, deserve
*eo, ire, i(v)i, itum	to go
*epistula -ae, f	letter
equidem	indeed, truly
*equus -i, m	horse
*ergo	therefore
Erinys, Erinyos, f	Fury (avenging spirit)
eripio, eripere, eripui, ereptum	to snatch, steal
*erro, errare, erravi, erratum	to go wrong, wander
*et	and
*ex (+ ablative)	out of
*excito, excitare, excitavi, excitatum	to awaken, arouse
exclamo, exclamare, exclamavi, exclamatum	to shout out aloud
excutio, excutere, excussi, excussum	to shake off
exeo, exire, exii, exitum	to go out of, leave
exhibeo, exhibere, exhibui, exhibitum	to show evidence
*expecto, expectare, expectavi, expectatum	to await, expect
exsilio, exsilire, exsilui	to jump up
exspes (nominative singular only)	hopeless
exul, exulis, f	exile
exulo, exulare, exulavi, exulatum	to be banished
facies -ei, f	face, form, appearance
*facinus, facinoris, n	deed
*facio, facere, feci, factum	to do, make
falsus -a -um	false, deceitful
falx, falcis, f	sickle, scythe
*fama -ae, f	report, rumour
fatum -i, n	fate, destiny
*faveo, favere, favi, fautum (+ dative)	to favour
fax, facis, f	torch
*felix, felicis	happy, fortunate
*femina -ae, f	woman
femineus -a -um	womanly

fera -ae, f	beast
*fero, ferre, tuli, latum	to carry, bear
fetus -ūs, m	offspring, children
*fides, fidei, f	faith, pledge
figo, figere, fixi, fixum	to pierce, transfix
figura -ae, f	shape
*filia -ae, f	daughter
*filius -i, m	son
filum -i, n	thread
fingo, fingere, finxi, fictum	to imagine
flecto, flectere, flexi, flectum	to bend
fleo, flere, flevi, fletum	to weep
*flumen, fluminis, n	river
fore = futurum esse (future infinitive of sum)	to be about to be
forem = essem (imperfect subjunctive of sum)	
forma -ae, f	shape, beauty
*fortis -e	brave, strong
*frater, fratris, m	brother
fraudo, fraudare, fraudavi, fraudatum (+ ablative)	to cheat out of
fraus, fraudis, f	deceit, trick
fretum -i, n	strait of the sea
frigidus -a -um	cold, freezing
frons, frontis, f	brow, forehead
fruor, frui, fructus sum (+ ablative; deponent verb)	to enjoy, make use of
frutex, fruticis, f	shrub, bush
*fuga -ae, f	flight
*fugio, fugere, fugi	to flee
fulvus -a -um	tawny, yellow in colour
furtum -i, n	theft, deceit
gemellus -i, m	twin
gemo, gemere, gemui, gemitum	to groan

gena -ae, f	eye, cheek
*genus, generis, n	class, species
germanus -a -um	sibling
glacies, glaciei, f	ice
grandis -e	great
*gratia -ae, f	influence, favour
gratulor, gratulari, gratulatus sum (deponent)	to congratulate
gravidus -a um	pregnant
*gravis -e	heavy
*habeo, habere, habui, habitum	to have
hactenus	so far
Haemonius -a -um	Thessalian
haereo, haerere, haesi, haesum	to stick to
harena -ae, f	sand
herba -ae, f	grass
heu	alas
*hic, haec, hoc	this
*hiems, hiemis,] f	winter, storm
*hinc	from here
hisco, hiscere	to gape open
*homo, hominis, m	human being
horreo, horrere, horrui	to shiver
*hospes, hospitis, m	visitor, foreigner
hostia -ae, f	sacrificial victim
*hostis -is, m	enemy
*huc	to this place
*humus -i, m	land, earth
Hymen	Hymen (God of Marriage)
Hypsipyle -es	Hypsipyle (Queen of Lemnos)
*iacio, iacere, ieci, iactum	to throw
iacto, iactare, iactavi, iactatum	to toss, hurl, boast
*iam	by now, already
Iason, Iasonis (accusative Iasona)	Jason

icio, icere, ici, ictum	to strike
*idem, eadem, idem	the same
iecur, iecoris, n	liver
ignavus -a -um	cowardly, faint-hearted
*ille, illa, illud	that
illuc	to that place
imber, imbris, m	rain shower
impello, impellere, impuli,	to push, drive
impulsum	
impleo, implere, implevi, impletum	to fill up
impono, imponere, imposui,	to attach to
impositum	
*in (+ accusative)	into, against
*in (+ ablative)	in, on
incertus -a um	uncertain
incolumis -e	safe
incumbo, incumbere, incubui,	to lie down
incubitum	
*inde	from then, from there
indignus -a -um	undeserving
infaustus -a -um	ill-omened
infelix, infelicis	unfortunate
*ingenium -i, n	skill
inhumatus -a -um	unburied
*iniquus -a -um	unfair
inmisceo, inmiscere, inmiscui,	to mix in with
inmixtum	
inops, inopis	helpless
inpavidus -a -um	fearless
insidior, insidiari, insidiatus sum	to ambush, plot against
(deponent)	
insimulo, insimulare,	to accuse, lay charges against
insimulavi, insimulatum	
*insula -ae, f	island
intepesco, intepescere, intepui	to become warm
*interea	meanwhile

*intro, intrare, intravi, intratum	to enter
*invenio, invenire, inveni, inventum	to find
*ipse, ipsa, ipsum	himself, herself, itself
*ira -ae, f	anger
iste, ista, istud	that
*ita	thus, in this way
*iterum	again
*itura (= feminine singular of the future participle of **eo**)	going to go
*iubeo, iubere, iussi, iussum	to order
iugum -i, n	yoke
Iuno, Iunonis	Juno (goddess)
Iuppiter, Iovis	Jupiter (god)
iuro, iurare, iuravi, iuratum	to swear an oath
ius, iuris, n	right, power
*iustus, -a, -um	just, right
labo, labare, labavi, labatum	to shake
*labor, labi, lapsus sum (deponent)	to glide, slip
lacero, lacerare, laceravi, laceratum	to tear to pieces
lacrima -ae, f	tear-drop
langueo, languere	to be sluggish, idle
languidus -a um	sluggish, slow
lapis, lapidis, m	stone
lassus -a -um	tired
late	far and wide
*latus -a -um	broad
lectulus -i, m	small bed
lectus -i, m	bed
*lego, legere, legi, lectum	to read
Lemnias, Lemniadis	a woman from Lemnos
Lemnos -i, f	the island of Lemnos
*lentus -a -um	sluggish, slow
letum -i, n	death
limen, liminis, n	threshold
*littera -ae, f	letter, writing

*litus, litoris, n	shore
*locus -i, m	place
*longus -a -um	long
*loquor, loqui, locutus sum (deponent)	to speak
lugeo, lugere, luxi, luctum	to mourn, grieve
lugubris -e	mournful
lumen, luminis, n	light, eye
luna -ae, f	moon
madeo, madere	to be wet
maereo, maerere	to grieve, be sad
maestus -a -um	sad
*magnus -a -um	big, great
*male (adverb)	badly
*maneo, manere, mansi, mansum	to stay, remain
mano, manare, manavi, manatum	to be wet
*manus -ūs, f	hand
*mare, maris, n	sea
marinus -a -um	of the sea
*maritus -i, m	husband
Mars, Martis, m	Mars (God of War)
*mater, matris, f	mother
Medea, Medeae	Medea
*melius (comparative adverb of **bonus**)	better
membrum -i, n	limb
memini, meminisse	to recall, remember
*mens, mentis, f	mind
meritum -i, n	meritorious act, kindness
messis, messis, f	harvest, crop
metior, metiri, mensus sum (deponent)	to survey
meto, metere, messui, messum	to reap, harvest
*metus -ūs, m	fear
*meus, mea, meum	my
*miles, militis, m	soldier
Minyae, -arum, m (plural)	descendants of Minyas, Thessalians

*miror, mirari, miratus sum	to admire, wonder at
misceo, miscere, miscui, mixtum	to mix
*miser, misera, miserum	wretched
mitis -e	gentle, sweet
*mitto, mittere, misi, missum	to send
*modo	only
mollis -e	soft, feminine
*mons, montis, f	mountain
*more (+ genitive)	in the manner of
*mos, moris, m	custom, rites
*morior, mori, mortuus sum	to die
(deponent)	
*moveo, movere, movi, motum	to move
mulceo, mulcere, mulsi, mulsum	to soothe
*nam	for
*narro, narrare, narravi, narratum	to narrate, tell a story
natus -i, m	son
*navita -ae, m (= nauta, -ae)	sailor
*ne	lest, to prevent, so that . . . not
*nec	nor, and not
*nego, negare, negavi, negatum	to deny, say that . . . not
nempe	of course
*nescio, nescire, nesci(v)i, nescitum	to not know
nex, necis, f	murder
*nil = nihil	nothing
nimium	too much
*nisi	unless, if . . . not
nitor, niti, nixus sum (deponent)	to strive
*noceo, nocere, nocui, nocitum	to harm
(+ dative)	
*nomen, nominis, n	name
*non	not
*nos, nostri	us
nosco, noscere, novi, notum	to get to know
*noster, nostra, nostrum	our

Notus -i,	south wind
noverca -ae, f	stepmother
*nox, noctis, f	night
*nullus -a -um,	not any, none
*numerus -i, m	number
*nunc	now
*nuntius -i, m	messenger
nuper	lately
nupta -ae, f	bride
nurus- ūs, f	daughter-in-law
nusquam	nowhere
o	o!
obliquus -a -um	coming at an angle
*obliviscor, oblivisci, oblitus sum (+ genitive, deponent)	to forget
obsequium -i, n	indulgence, kindness
obsum, obesse, obfui	to obstruct
obvius -a -um	obstructing
occido, occidere, occidi, occasum	to perish, die
*oculus -i, m	eye
*officium -ii, n	duty
Ogygius -a -um	Theban
*omnis -e	all
*oportet (impersonal verb)	it is right
oppositus -a -um	facing, opposite
*ops, opis, f	help (plural: wealth)
*ora -ae, f	shore,
orbs, orbis, f	world
orbus -a -um (+ genitive)	bereaved
*ordo, ordinis, f	order
*oro, orare, oravi, oratum	to beg, ask
*os, oris, f	face, mouth
os, ossis, n	bone
*ostendo, ostendere, ostendi, ostensum	to show
ovis, ovis, f	sheep

pabulum -i, n	food, fodder
pacisco, paciscere, pactum	to agree, promise
paco, pacare, pacavi, pacatum	to make peaceful
paelex, paelicis, f	mistress
palma -ae, f	palm (of the hand)
pandus -a -um	curved, bent
*parco, parcere, peperci (+ dative)	to spare
*parens, parentis, m	parent
*pario, parere, peperi, partum	to produce, get
*pars, partis, f	part
*passus -ūs, m	footstep
*pater, patris, m	father
paternus -a -um	fatherly
*patior, pati, passus sum (deponent)	to suffer, allow
*patria, -ae, f	fatherland
pectus, pectoris, n	chest, breast
pecus, pecudis, n	sheep, animal
*peius (= comparative adverb from malus)	worse
*pello, pellere, pepuli, pulsum	to drive
pendeo, pendere, pependi	to hang, be suspended
*per (+ accusative)	through
*perdo, perdere, perdidi, perditum	to lose, destroy
peregrinus -a -um	foreign
perfidia, -ae, f	treachery
perfidus -a -um	treacherous
*periculum -i, n	danger
perimo, perimere, peremi, peremptum	to destroy
periurus -a -um	false, lying
persolvo, persolvere, persolvi, persolutum	to fulfil (a vow)
pervigilis, -e	unsleeping
*pes, pedis, m	foot
pignus, pignoris, n	pledge
pinus, -ūs, f	pine

Pittheis, Pittheidos, f	daughter of Pittheus
pius -a -um	dutiful, good
***placet** (impersonal verb)	it pleases, it seems good
plango, plangere, planxi, planctum	to beat the breast
plangor -oris, m	beating the breast
plus (comparative adverb from **multus**)	more
***poena -ae, f**	punishment, penalty
***pono, ponere, posui, positum**	to set in position, place
***populus -i, m**	people, nation
***portus, -ūs, f**	port harbour
***possum, posse, potui**	to be able
***postquam** (conjunction)	after
***potius** (adverb)	rather
praeceps, praecipitis	falling headlong
praecipito, praecipitare, praecipitavi, praecipitatum	to hurl headlong
praefero, praeferre, praetuli, praelatum	to carry forward
praepono, praeponere, praeposui, praepositum	to prefer
***praeter** (+ accusative)	past
preces, precum (f.pl.)	prayers
premo, premere, pressi, pressum	to press down upon
prendo, prendere, prendi, prensum	to grasp, take hold of
***pretium -i, n**	reward
primo (adverb)	at first
primum (adverb)	at first
***prior, prius** (comparative)	earlier
***pro** (+ ablative)	for, on behalf of
procer, proceris, m	chief, leading man
***prodo, prodere, prodidi, proditum**	to betray, hand over
profundo, profundere, profudi, profusum	to pour out
***promitto, promittere, promisi, promissum**	to promise
pronuba -ae, f	matron of honour (at wedding)

propello, propellere, propulsi, propulsum	to drive onwards
prospectus -ūs, m	view, prospect
prospicio, prospicere, prospexi, prospectum	to look out on
protinus	immediately
pruina -ae, f	dew, hoar-frost
pudicus -a -um	chaste, modest
*pudor, pudoris, m	modesty, shame
puellaris, -e	girlish
*puer, pueri, m	boy
pulso, pulsare, pulsavi, pulsatum	to beat, batter against
puppis -is, f	(stern of a) ship
*puto, putare, putavi, putatum	to think
*quaero, quaerere, quaesivi, quaesitum	to ask, seek
*qualis, -e	what sort of
*quam	how, than
quamlibet (with adjective)	however much
*quantus -a -um	how great
*queror, queri, questus sum (deponent)	to complain, lament
*qui, quae, quod (relative pronoun)	who, what
*quia	because
*quid	what?
*quidem	indeed
*quod	because
*quoniam	since
*quoque	also
*quotiens	how often
*rapio, rapere, rapui, raptum	to take, seize
rarus -a -um	isolated, rare
ratis -is, f	boat
raucus -a -um	rough
*recipio, recipere, recepi, receptum	to receive, welcome

recursus -ūs, f	return
recurvus -a -um	bent back, curved
*reddo, reddere, reddidi, redditum	to give back
*redeo, redire, redii, reditum	to go back, return
redux, reducis	returning
*refero, referre, rettuli, relatum	to bring back
refreno, refrenare, refrenavi, refrenatum	to curb, restrain
regia -ae, f	royal seat
regno, regnare, regnavi, regnatum	to reign, rule
*regnum -i, n	kingdom
*rego, regere, rexi, rectum	to rule over
relabor, relabi, relapsus sum (deponent)	to slide back
*relinquo, relinquere, reliqui, relictum	to leave, abandon
reluctor, reluctari, reluctatus sum (deponent)	to wrestle against, be unwilling
repeto, repetere, repeti(v)i, repetitum	to seek again
repleo, replere, replevi, repletum	to fill back up again
requiro, requirere, requisi(v)i, requisitum	to ask for, seek out
*res, rei, f	thing, matter
retempto, retemptare, retemptavi, retemptatum	to try again
reverto, revertere, reverti, reversum	to turn back
*rogo, rogare, rogavi, rogatum	to ask
rogus -i, m	funeral pyre
*rumpo, rumpere, rupi, ruptum	to tear, dishevel, break
sacer, sacra, sacrum	holy
*saepe	often
saltem	at least
*salus, salutis, f	safety
salvus -a -um	safe

sanguinolentus -a -um	blood-stained
*sanguis -is, m	blood
saxeus, saxea, saxeum	rocky
saxum -i, n	rock
sceleratus -a -um	criminal
*scelus, sceleris, n	crime
scilicet	doubtless, of course
scopulus -i, m	rock, cliff-face
*scribo, scribere, scripsi, scriptum	to write
*se (reflexive pronoun)	himself, herself, itself, themselves
seco, secare, secavi, secatum	to cut
securus -a -um	carefree, secure
*sed	but
*sedes, sedis, f	seat, abode
seges, segetis, f	crops
semen, seminis, n	seed
semianimis, -e	half-dead
semisupinus -a -um	half upright
*semper	always
*senex, senis, m	old man
*sentio, sentire, sensi, sensum	to feel
sepelio, sepelire, sepeli(v)i, sepelitum	to bury
sepulcrum -i, n	tomb
*sequor, sequi, secutus sum (deponent)	to follow
serpens, serpentis, m or f	snake
serta -ae, f	garland
*servo, servare, servavi, servatum	to save, preserve
*si	if
si quid	if any
*sicut	just as if
signo, signare, signavi, signatum	to seal (a letter)
*signum -i, n	sign
silens, silentis	silent
*silva -ae, f	wood, forest
simulacrum -i, n	image, model

*sine	without
singulus -a -um	individual
*sino, sinere, sivi, situm	to allow
sinus, -ūs, m	lap, bosom
*socius -i, m	ally
*sol, solis, m	sun
*solus -a -um	alone
*somnus -i, m	sleep
sono, sonare, sonui, sonitum	to make a sound
sospes, sospitis	safe and sound, unscathed
spargo, spargere, sparsi, sparsum	to sprinkle, scatter
spectabilis -e,	available to view
*specto, spectare, spectavi, spectatum	to look at
*spes, spei, f	hope, expectation
spiritus -ūs, m	breath, spirit
*spolium -i, n	spoil, hide
*sto, stare, steti, statum	to stand
stratum -i, n	coverlet, blanket
*studium -i, n	enthusiasm
*sub	under
subduco, subducere, subduxi, subductum	to draw away from under
*subito	suddenly
subnuba -ae, f	substitute bride
subripio, subripere, surripui, surreptum	to steal
*sum, esse, fui	to be
*summus -a -um	highest, top of
*sumo, sumere, sumpsi, sumptum	to take
*supero, superare, superavi, superatum	to remain
supersto, superstare, superstiti	to hover over
*surgo, surgere, surrexi, surrrectum	to arise
*suus, sua, suum (reflexive possessive adjective)	his, her, its

taeda -ae, f	wedding-torch, wedding
*talis, tale	of such a kind
*tam	so
*tamen	however
*tango, tangere, tetigi, tactum	to touch
tardo, tardare, tardavi, tardatum	to slow down
taurus -i, m	bull
*tectum -i, n	construction, building
*tecum	with you
*tego, tegere, texi, tectum	to cover over, conceal
tellus, telluris, f	earth, land
temerarius -a -um	rash, hot-headed
tempero, temperare, temperavi, temperatum	to regulate, restrain
*templum -i, n	temple
tempora -um, n (plural)	temples (of the head)
tempto, temptare, temptavi, temptatum	to attempt, try
tendo, tendere, tetendi, tentum	to stretch
tenebrae, tenebrarum, f (plural)	darkness, shadows
*teneo, tenere, tenui, tentum	to hold, keep
tenuis -e	thin
tepidus -a -um	warm
*terra -ae, f	earth
terrigenus -a -um	born of earth
*tertius -a -um	third
testis -is, m/f	witness
thalamus -i, m	bedroom, chamber
Theseus (accusative: Thesea)	Theseus
Thessalia -ae, f	Thessaly
Thessalus -a -um	Thessalian
Thoantias	daughter of Thoas
Thoas, Thoantos	Thoas, father of Hypsipyle
*timeo, timere, timui	to fear
timidus -a -um	fearful
*timor, timoris, m	fear

Tiphys	Tiphys (helmsman of the Argo)
titulus -i, m	inscription
torpeo, torpere	be lethargic
torus -i, m	marriage-bed
totidem	as many
totiens	so many times, so often
***totus -a -um**	all of, whole
***traho, trahere, traxi, tractum**	to drag, attract
***trans** (+ accusative)	across
tremens, trementis	trembling
***tristis, -e**	sad
Tritonis, Tritonidos	belonging to Pallas Athena
***tu**	you
tueor, tueri (deponent)	to protect, watch over
***tum**	then
tumeo, tumere	swell
tumulus -i, m	mound
tunica -ae, f	tunic
***turba -ae, f**	crowd
turbidus -a -um	disordered
turpis, -e	disgraceful
turris -is, f	tower
***tutus -a -um**	safe
***tuus -a -um**	your
***ubi**	where
***ullus**	any
***ultimus -a -um**	last, furthest
***unda -ae, f**	wave
***unde**	from where
unguo, unguere, unxi, unctum	to anoint
***unus, una, unum**	one
***urbs, urbis, f**	city
urgeo, urgere, ursi	press, push
***ut**	so that, when, as, though
***uterque, utraque, utrumque**	each of the two

utinam	would that
*utor, uti, usus sum (+ ablative, deponent)	to use
utroque	in both directions
*uxor, uxoris, f	wife
vaco, vacare, vacavi, vacatum (+ ablative)	to be empty, devoid of
vagus, vaga, vagum	roaming, wandering freely
velamen, velaminis, n	clothing, covering
vellus, velleris, n	fleece
velum -i, n	sail
venefica -ae, f	female poisoner
veneficium -ii, n	poisoning
venenum -i, n	poison
*venio, venire, veni, ventum	to come
*ventus -i, m	wind
verber, verberis, n	blow, punch
*verbum -i, n	word
*vereor, vereri, veritus sum (deponent)	to fear
vertex, verticis, m	summit
*verto, vertere, verti, versum	to turn
vestigium -i, n	footprint
*via -ae, f	road, route
*victor, victoris, m	victor
*video,videre, vidi, visum	to see
viduus -a -um	bereaved
vigilo, vigilare, vigilavi, vigilatum	to be awake
villus -i, m	shaggy tuft of hair
vincio, vincire, vinxi, vinctum	to bind, wreathe
*vinco, vincere, vici, victum	to defeat
vipereus -a -um	belonging to vipers/snakes
*vir, viri, m	man
virga -ae, f	stick
virgo, virginis, f	unmarried girl
*vis, vim, f	strength, power

*vita -ae, f	life
vitreus -a -um	glassy
*vivo, vivere, vixi, victum	to live
*vivus -a -um	alive
*vix	scarcely
vix, vicis, f	turn
*voco, vocare, vocavi, vocatum	to call
volo, volare, volavi, volatum	to fly
*volo, velle, volui	to want
volucris -is, f	bird
votum -i, n	vow
*vox, vocis, f	voice
*vulnus, vulneris, n	wound
*vultus -ūs, f	facial expression